JIMI HENDRIX
CHEROKEE MIST

THE LOST WRITINGS

JIMI HENDRIX
CHEROKEE MIST

THE LOST WRITINGS

COMPILED AND EDITED BY BILL NITOPI

HarperPerennial

A Division of HarperCollins*Publishers*

CHEROKEE MIST: THE LOST WRITINGS OF JIMI HENDRIX

Compiled and edited by Bill Nitopi

ASSISTANT EDITOR Charles Blass
PROJECT CONSULTANT AND CONTRIBUTING EDITOR Michael Fairchild
RESEARCH COORDINATOR Tony Brown
PHOTOGRAPH RESEARCH ASSISTANT Andrew Hawley
PROJECT CONTRIBUTORS Monika Dannemann, Wayne Rodgers

Letters, unpublished lyrics and poems written by Jimi Hendrix included in
this book are published with the kind permission of Bella Godiva Music, Inc.

A hardcover edition of this book was published in 1993 by HarperCollins Publishers.

HarperCollins books may be purchased for educational, business, or
sales promotional use. For information, please write: Special Markets Department,
HarperCollins Publishers, Inc., 10 East 53rd Street, New York, NY 10022.

First HarperPerennial edition published 1994.

DESIGNED BY HELENE BERINSKY

The Library of Congress has catalogued the hardcover edition as follows:

Hendrix, Jimi
Cherokee mist : the lost writings of Jimi Hendrix / by Jimi Hendrix ;
edited by Bill Nitopi.
p. cm.
Principally poems, lyrics, and photographs.
ISBN 0-06-016976-1
1. Hendrix, Jimi. I. Nitopi, Bill. II. Title.
ML410.H476A25   1993
787.87'166'092—dc20   92-56231   MN

ISBN 0-06-092562-0 (pbk.)
94 95 96 97 98 DT/CW 10 9 8 7 6 5 4 3 2 1

To all the people who can actually feel and think for themselves,
and feel free for themselves.

CONTENTS

(Bill Nitopi Collection)

APPRECIATION

J ust a few years ago I made a pilgrimage with some guitar magazine colleagues from the civilized metropolis of New York to the
wild environs of New Jersey to meet with a legend, a guy who,
according to the hype was the ultimate repository for Hendrixiana.
Stoked on the euphoria of the moment, we roared down the highway to search through the files of one Bill Nitopi. Files which con-
tained not only every poster imaginable of Hendrix concerts and
trips, but detailed visual evidence of Nitopi's supreme effort and
lifelong obsession, the search for and chronicling of photographs
rare and exceptional of Mr. Hendrix, and chronicles that chronicled
the chronicling of the ultimate chronicle.

The Oracle. That's what he was to our mind's eye, as we crept
up the rickety stairs to his sixties-cum-college-roommate decor.

A crabby young man greeted us, suspicious as all hell about what
these representatives of big city publishing were up to, snooping
around in his files, asking questions. They said they were from *Guitar World,* all right, a magazine known for its editor's penchant for
enshrining things. Things like '59 Strats and Les Pauls. Bill had
stories of unscrupulous collectors, people who'd sat at Al Hendrix's
feet, waiting till he was distracted and then scooping up valuable
correspondence from Jimi.

But these guys weren't that way. The editor was talking about
this humongous tribute to Jimi he was planning, *The Unpublished
Hendrix,* and how cool it would be and how it would seek to compile

all these previously unseen photos of Jimi. Nitopi couldn't resist—these guys were all right. The next thing you knew, they were all on the floor, oohs and aahs sputtering. The rare sequence of Jimi rolling around on the floor with his Strat; the Joe Sia shot of the ravished Marshalls with the haunting shadow of Jimi; the meticulous chronicling of pictures of Jimi with other axes bold as love: the Black Vs and the acoustic twelve; and the ultimate sleuthing job Bill pulled off by doggedly approaching documentary filmmaker Albert Maysles to unveil his outtakes from *Gimme Shelter,* showing backstage jamming by Hendrix, Keith Richards, Mick Jagger, and Mick Taylor.

The inhospitable oracle soon became an indefatigable researcher, collaborator and friend to this beleaguered editor of *Guitar World* magazine, and we soon had much to show for the fruits of our collaboration—*The Unpublished Hendrix* belied its name and was indeed published to the cheers of Hendrix collectors everywhere, and it became the single most popular issue in *Guitar World*'s history.

And now, Nitopi has gone much further. Not content to rest on his laurels and finger his personal copies of our mammoth publishing collaboration, the Topester kept on collecting, uncovering some of the gems you see reproduced on the pages of this book. Nitopi dug under every rock and found new evidence, new pieces of the Grail. He'd find some obscure underground newspaper from 1969 that only printed a thousand copies to begin with, and notice a photo credit he wasn't familiar with from the coterie of much-mined Hendrix photographers. The concert was at the Washington Hilton, Nitopi deduced. He'd follow the trail past local phone books and unlikely sources, coming up with a fashion photographer in D.C. who didn't need the money or the fame, but was somehow touched by Nitopi's bid to become a part of History. The fashion photographer produced eight rolls of immaculate shots of Hendrix in performance that had never been developed.

Aside from photographic footprints of the deity, Bill has gathered together some of the artifacts, pages from Hendrix's life, like the pages and pages of poetry that Hendrix produced constantly on airplane napkins and hotel stationery. It is all lovingly reproduced here.

I am certainly looking forward to reading this book and cherishing it. And when you do, you'll see why Bill is no longer the curmudgeonly collector, but the enlightened curator, sharing the wisdom he has so soulfully gained.

—NoË GOLD
Founding Editor of *Guitar World* and
Editorial Director of the Hendrix Estate

EDITOR'S NOTE

In early spring of 1980 my friend Chip Stern wrote an article for the *Village Voice* reviewing the new Jimi Hendrix album, *Nine to the Universe*. Accompanying this article was a magnificent picture of Jimi taken by photo artist Nona Hatay. It was here that I began to contact photographers through the elementary observation and researching of photo credits. Meeting and becoming close friends with Nona Hatay sparked me on to a thirteen-year nonstop road of research into the life of Jimi Hendrix, someone I already knew very well. I became a magnet for Hendrix photos, at times feeling that I had been mysteriously steered down a road that wasn't on the map, there to find a new picture and a new friend. It has been an honor to unearth new pictures and also to find that a few photographers also shot movie film—adding to the honor of finding new photos the thrilling experience of discovering raw film footage! After years of intense research and five *major* film discoveries, I then understood how it must have felt for Howard Carter to research, discover, and unearth the tomb of King Tut.

After a decade of contributing Hendrix photos to over two dozen publications, I now present to you here the cream of the crop. Along with the greatest photographs the world has ever seen, it is with the deepest and most sincere respect that I am able to publish here for the first time a virtual treasure chest of Jimi's handwritten lyrics, essays, and letters.

Finally the world has a book on Jimi Hendrix, written by the only person qualified to do so—himself.

My friend Chris Doering once wrote:

> The story of Jimi Hendrix will never be told, because nobody knows it. It's impossible to find the traces of a living person in the published remembrances of the players who worked or jammed with him, and the girls who slept with him, as if those who shared his time and space were unable or unwilling to look inside that divine/demonic image and, by recognizing him, allow the man who *had* to live there a moment's freedom. The story of the man is lost, and the stories of the image lose a little interest every time they're retold. But the music remains, nourishing and sustaining those of us who like to feel a little bit more human sometimes. The music has its own stories to tell, and unlike the image, it hasn't lost its power.

To this, allow me to add that every book thus far released on Jimi Hendrix has failed miserably in capturing his spirit, mostly because of gypsy authors who attempt to set records straight while they fatten their wallets. Authors who can somehow slide under any doorway and slither through any crack in order to be heard and get their books published. These long-winded authors are better qualified to milk goats rather than to write books. But, in keeping with the spirit of *this* book, I'd like now to thank the friends who helped me do a lot of work.

First I must thank my old high school buddy, Mark Landau, who is almost singlehandedly responsible for getting me off my lazy ass and out of bed in order that I do this book.

Also due a huge credit and thanks is Craig Nelson, who helped me along the road to getting this book accepted by HarperCollins.

Next I'd like to thank my work force, who have done a tremendous job at helping me with all this work: Charles Blass, Michael Fairchild, Monika Dannemann, Alan Douglas, Don Williams, Tony Brown, Andrew Hawley, Wayne Rodgers, Klaus-Peter Dannemann, Barry Gruber, Dave Pearcy, Joe Sia, Steve Roby, Noë Gold, Virginia Lohle, Paul Donato, Juma Sultan, Tamara and everyone at Crystal Color, Tom Frye, Diane Serratore, Mark Albert, Larry Graham, Jim

Nadel, Brian Doyle, Lou Schwartz, Ron Plotkin, Sue Schneider, Nancy Carter, Mike Quashie, Steve Routhier, Tony Gerard, Herbert Worthington, Peter Irwin, Larry Fisher, Mike Casady, John Bellissimo, Jaycaber Kastor, Kevin Stein, Lauren Marino, Danny Toan, Zeb Burgess, Tomas Sandströn, Robert Beerbohm, Billy Perry, Al Hendrix, Jeff Levy—and a big thanks to my family for supporting me and for putting up with all my shit.

A warm thank you goes out to Enya for making the most beautiful music I've ever heard.

I dedicate this book to the memory of my dear friends, Stevie Ray Vaughan and Jack Plotkin, War Heroes.

—BILL NITOPI

SEND MY LOVE TO LINDA

Send my love to you
I'm sending all my love to you
Send my love to Linda
She lit a fire way down inside
She made the sun shine in my eye
God let me hold her once more before I die.

—JIMI HENDRIX

Saville Theatre, London, January 27, 1967 (Tony Gale/Starfile)

PREFACE

in these words some may search for color . . . for hope to clouds of Joy . . .
But that is a road on to its own . . . it may go in circles . . . and you
may wind up, by it, only to be painfully employed.

With a wink, Kingdoms, Fables and worlds unfold . . .

HAUNTING UTOPIAN ELEGIES

You hold a mine of Black Gold, a fountain of essential rare glimpses
and panoramas, twenty-three years silent in page-capsules of sus-
pended animation. It is uncanny to fathom the depths of James
Marshall Hendrix, the out-of-time timeliness of his efforts verbal
and nonverbal. His is a sublime synthesis, a spark that fuses together
races, generations, dimensions. Here is previously withheld evidence
of his herculean African-Cherokee-Irish-American achievements.

Jimi Hendrix is an iceberg pyramid rearing its tip, tongue aimed
and loaded, waiting to shoot again into space. His true nature has
been widely ignored in the mainstream, eclipsed by his sheer power
and lurid hype. We aim here to present some clear pictures, necessary
bigger pictures.

The words are indeed in the master's pen, but the nature of these
particular achievements is inevitably "unauthorized." Hendrix was
not around in the flesh to edit this compilation. The sharpness of
Jimi's tragedy has not dulled over two short decades; perhaps it cuts
yet deeper with musical and political hindsight.

Open to any page—there is no correct order. Each shifting thought and feeling sweeps a chain of interchangeable links. We've attempted to breathe life back into the body of words Jimi left us, to sort the pieces in some chronological and conceptual fashion. Relative adherence to the clock molds an autobiography, a mirroring of Jimi's linear path through this realm.

Most of our work was done for us. The pieces placed themselves as movements in Jimi's grand symphony. But he was not alone in a creative bubble. Jimi Hendrix mirrored everyone and everything at once, with every atom of his being. Instantly ambidextrous, he was able to play right- and left-handed guitars *and* grasp musical phrases backward and forward. He is a virtual hologram of mirrors: *"Don't be afraid of me—for I am you."*

We cannot know how Jimi would react to this publication. Perfectionism challenged him to continual revision. Self-critical, self-conscious, and self-indulgent, his output is extremely *private*. His management and his role as a popular performing artist forced the development, modification, and/or completion of many poem-songs, a necessary translation or valve to a deeper, unknowable flow. Neither is his sense of nonsense to be denied. Jimi's many-tongued Joker is wild, cutting, shuffling, with fingers dealing hands from many sleeves. Hendrix pushed limits of form in all spheres: sonic, linguistic, socio-religio-kitch'n-sync.

These works in progress allow us to hear the voices within Jimi Hendrix. His imagery is fantastic, still moving, focused and relevant, his scope awesome and razor-clear. Subsequent or alternate versions of some titles differ drastically from the original or "official," indicating (along with spontaneous edits) a continuous flux within and between each piece. Here is much lyrical honing and polishing, pruning the thick overgrowth of Free Soul.

Coupled with his music and physical presence, the impact of Jimi's words is more immediate; but removed from their intended context they deliver no less. Hendrix's brushstrokes are bold and raw, conceived and executed with purity of intention and epic-erotic Hollywood enigma. His screenplays are sketches of reference to abstractions made concrete by the voice of his guitar.

Jimi's literacy was more aural than letter-perfect; his grammar and spelling are not from the classroom. Meaning always comes through, though at times precognitive (like the curiously repeated misspelling of *guide* as *guild*). Punctuation is the funky rhythm, periods stretching and blending into ellipses, dashes, and squiggles. Here we have some prototypical, archetypal mytho-scatological rap poetry: Above all of his wire techniques, M.C. Jimi was plugged into The Groove, receiving, transmitting, repeating long and rapid thrusts of gnosis. Despite unlikely separation from the music, his words are fresh beats and rhymes for the times, drops of Science between the lines.

These writings further propel Hendrix beyond the world of pop music, underscoring his preeminence in modern culture. His style spirals DNA-ribbons, recalls past lives of Egyptian princes, snaps elemental Delta fingers, flames licking sparks of southern preachers' tongues, flipping dimensional pages of sci-fi and newsprint comics. The move to England was crucial; Jimi absorbed the echoes of centuries of nuance and inflection. He has a refreshing capacity for history and politics, and, contrary to common opinion, he *did* respond directly to the factions of his day. He demonstrates a scathing perspective which has been selectively magnified by the media game in its attempt to snatch freeze-frames from motion pictures of a departing comet. The flag of Hendrix unfurls, revealing Jimi as a consummate space/time-traveling Renaissance man.

Hendrix was chained to the nonstop ball of a civilization at the peak of promiscuity, spiritual revival entwined with inebriant mania. The flowering animation of Jimi's handwriting confesses passions of untapped potential, and simultaneous illusion. Ark-ancient and modern, natural and synthetic fabrics of a tie-dye eyelid-silkscreen Reality come in and out of vogue, shifting the velocity and altitude of a soul's course.

In this undeniably addictive society, too many messages mix from all directions. Cocktails of crushed, frozen notions melt as signals shake and stir. Party lines cross and scramble; spasms and convulsions are constantly caused and cured; "medicine" and "biochemistry" are words, but defined by and for whom? Which doctor do we call?

"*. . . your world turns to nothing but a bubble . . .*" Certain molecules, hinting amino-mysteries Eleusinian, bypass ego to erase and reset pre-programmed autopilot filters, opening chutes above

Jimi Hendrix underwent extensive U.S.-certified flight and jump training; later, the gravitation of a sleepless rock 'n' roll free-fall would crank levels to screaming Blue Yonder. (It is useless to suppose that meditation, self-defense, or earplugs could have navigated his meteor through the tempest.)

To the broken hearts, minds, and bodies of the fearful pestilential city, Jimi urges movement away. One facet of his tragedy is that he left his neck open to many of that city's vampires and ever-tightening nooses. (And he paraded, banners waving across the globe, looping, embroidering the knots in shimmering colors.) He was staggeringly prolific, yet much of his finest work remains unknown. "Ownership," "copyright," and other terms may apply to the soul of a man, alive or dead, in bittersweet covenant. Sadly, the most powerful force over blood on this planet is money—veined in name by Gold, inked on walls of dusty parchment dungeons.

All posthumously released Jimi Hendrix material seems forbidden, given his premature and forever controversial transition. But his Message, very much alive, has had some time to ripen in the aftermath of that sudden loss. Vast legions of guitarists surfing his awesome wake send a sonic boom round the planet, but very few have taken that wave beyond the Stratosphere to reach Jimi's ears. Shells opening sesame, many pearls are disclosed as collectors and fans diving around Atlantis paw through traces of his bones filtered across the briny decades. But the best pearls are not flawless. For all Jimi's supernatural qualities, his fossils contain plenty of human error. Some are approximations, hints of shining gems to follow. Most, however, remain diamonds into eternity.

There are dangers in trying to see through Jimi. Blindness and confusion are pitfalls beside the road which lies Straight Ahead. His earthly person was brought forth under specific circumstances, with specific results. One thing is absolute: Jimi Hendrix had much *experience,* and his writing and playing are direct transmissions of his True Life. Jimi Hendrix lived his own Gospel.

One's eyes light readily on Woman: cornerstones of Hendrix's being, whether as angel or devil, witch or bitch, wife, mother, or baby of the universe—she is his "other half," in fact "the whole ½ of today."

Jimi's intensely personal and profound insights chip away at worn-out notions of "Love." ". . . *don't rely on no man—to try and understand—*" Reflections of Jimi's women bring into focus motivations of, and convergences and dichotomies between, his human and superhuman aspects.

"She has the devil in her eye and holds an angel in her heart . . . She'll get you wrapped around her little finger and tear your mind a million miles apart. . . Her Kiss is a cup of Sunshine. . . ." Jimi Hendrix stands on the verge of an enticing minefield, pain and pleasure gazing at each other. "Hell to Heaven/Heaven to Hell/Please send Devil or Angel/to Love me *NOW.*/to Hell with Heaven/to Heaven with Hell." On the flip side of that envelope, Jimi wrote "I'll never fall in Love . . ." Paradise tossed, who knows which side came first?

Jimi Hendrix observes the planet through a child's eyes, asking a child's questions: "Why have not these wars and scars . . . long before come to pass?" He performed primarily for children, radiating: "Power to the people, freedom of the soul—Pass it on to the young and old." Public and private, sectors of age are the "Different States of America." Earth's changing faces speak of hopeful futures bought and sold on the killing floors of the global "Roman Empire U.S.A." Greedy circuits oversaturate with the momentum of consumption, choking on rotten industrial glut. Empty-white megabyte corporations crash in molten microchip nightmares of tumbling black letters and numbers; cardhouse museums collapse in a "royal change of the rubble," ashen plagues coughing Virus as another modality of Jimi's genius.

"As long as you want to believe the world is a stage, then appoint me, your electric stagehand . . . and I shall produce upon you an overwhelming hurricane . . . straight from your own script . . ." Jimi Hendrix's gifts are made manifest over and over in the form of prophesy. Curious numerology and scenes of devastation are viewed through Belly Button Window's tinted telescope. Glowing spaceship portals and computer screens' "EXP" forecast the crowning of "Mother Moon" as "Crystal Ball" ("just a flash from my memory . . ."). In Jimi's grand helter-skelter scheme, the orbits of the races of Atlantis, Earth and "the chain of the space rocks" collide as God recalibrates the clockwork of the cosmos.

Angel transmits celestial knowledge "about the Love between

the moon and the sea—" but that Love, reflective and magnetic, can entrap. The Moon, as Sun's Mirror, clutches "spinning slave pebble Earth" in shadowy tides of emotion. Lunatic energy surrounding him, Jimi spent most nights up with the moon, howling feedback to the skies. Moon reigns over change, the waters of consciousness, but at the end of the night, the spotlight is definitely On: The Star of the Show is the New Rising Sun—casting Neptune, Venus and others in the wings.

Much of Jimi's work, increasingly so toward the end of his life, renders itself in the form of sermons and prayers. This book might be considered an Electric Church prayerbook of Jimi Hendrix. His zen-cupid arrows pierce the quivering heart of his Muse, sizzle through the bull's-eye of his Mandala, whiz past his presence toward an idyll of tomorrow's Rainbow. Master of Ceremony, Hendrix whispers Secrets of Sound with radical-evangelist fervor and collected, informed authority, on the One.

There are connections and references to Jesus Christ throughout the life of Hendrix. Jimi had a strong awareness of this affinity; his are pastoral dreams and shepherd visions. More than most, Jimi Hendrix can be proclaimed a Gypsy Messiah of our wandering ages. He resisted this mantle, though at times unconvinced and unconvincing, with his parabolic shield of parables. "Then all of a sudden Jesus took on through the Mirror just ahead of me . . . I realized that he was as spaced out as me." But, Jimi answers, "I sure ain't you." In "Forget of My Name," Jimi lashes out at man's "questionable timid compromises . . . which I will erase. Without hint of reward as I am only a messenger. And you a sheep in process of evolution." Jimi bore his cross over many roads, but did he demand reimbursement? Whether he considered it reward or punishment, Hendrix got paid vastly more than other performers of his day. Perhaps at this point of Return lies the crux of his Condescension-Ascension.

"EXIT; stage down in forgetful History. . . ." Jimi is so aligned with a realm beyond; his prophecies are perhaps most overt in reference to his own death. "The Earth gives and takes away/But my soul will outlive any black day." Was Jimi Hendrix a martyr or engineer of his fate? "I wanna keep on livin' . . . I wanna be alive when I die." Fresh-brewed debate percolates as insufficient data supports opposing conspiracy. Interpretation of his lines—all are speculative judgments. Many fingers are pointed, many hands were involved. "I gotta leave this town . . ."

Jimi's Armageddon, ejecting tombstones and brimstones, is his Mirror-Miracle-Oracle-Odyssey played back through techno-tapestries' endless spools twisting dizzy, tangling cables despite feeble attempts to control by knobs and buttons. "Music at this point shall scorch the audience. . . . The colors will be reds, oranges, burning colors. Moving and changing patterns." Treaded flickering celluloid, Jimi Hendrix's insight was outtasight, not chrono-logic but Real-To-Real: he was a "War Child," born a man, died a child.

"The Story of Life" is fertile ground for the plunder of exegesis. In reverence to the Creator, Jimi Hendrix vowed "Faith in the Beat," pulsing breath of yin-yang. Jimi is a voyager across the chasms, leaping light-years which pretend to separate young and old, earth and space, hell and heaven . . . woman and man. "This time with a woman in our arms" is Hendrix's hailed deathbed reversal of the Mary myth. "LOVE" is ultimately his Message, a higher Beauty— "SO TRUE you know that heaven is DEEP within you . . ." The final Word, distilled and extracted through the perfect laboratory of his life, is dynamic *not* static. This is no ordinary experience. The Jimi Hendrix Experience *is* Making Love—vibrations of living, gasping Physical Love.

"There should be no questions
there should be no lies."

"Now the whole world is here for me to see."

Peace and happiness to Lisa Blass, Jimi Hendrix, Billy Cox, Sherlock Nitopi, Michael Fairchild, Barry Gruber, Paul Caruso, Eddie Hazel/ P-Funk, Le Son'y Ra, analog and digital labyrinths, and proofreaders everywhere, WKCR-FM (89.9) NYC, family, and untold loved ones, You.

—CHARLES BLASS
New York City, 1993

(Nona Hatay)

INTRODUCTION

J imi Hendrix played guitar with his left hand and wrote script with his right. His dual-circuitry brain seemed to straddle mutually exclusive realms. With one ear in this world and one in the next, Jimi was tuned to a union of polarities. His life and art united contradictions: spiritual/physical, black/white, poverty/wealth, patriot/rebel, pacifist/soldier, hi-tech/natural, orchestral/solo, rhythm/ lead, primitive/futuristic, practical/idealist, shy/bold, masculine/ feminine, hippie/elite, ugly/beautiful, commercial/underground. Everything Jimi touched bears fantastic imprints of a consummate individualist. His art is so outstanding because his senses and perceptions stood so *outside* of *ordinary* limits.

Ever present with Hendrix is the *unexpected* twist; we hear it in his solos, we feel it in his harmonies, we see it in his wardrobe, we respond to it in his quotes, we watch it in his stageplay and we read it in his writings. Jimi operated from a psychological position of intense mystery and appeal.

After his death on September 18, 1970, his dwellings were ransacked. Untold treasures were confiscated. Like fragments from a deepsea wreck, slowly over the decades this booty has surfaced for ransom on the black market and in prestigious auction houses. From December 1990 to December 1991, three major sales dredged up a watershed of Jimi's original handwritings. When added to the pages that had already been gathered during the '70s and '80s, Hendrix experts were stunned by the most amazing archaeological find since the unearthing of the Dead Sea Scrolls. Like emotions frozen on paper, the nooks and crannies of Jimi's psyche stared back at us from beneath the ice. These writings offer a view from within akin to the first Viking probe's transmitted pictures from the surface of Mars. Finally we see with clarity areas that have previously appeared so obscure.

When reading Jimi's script, we see pages he regarded as highly personal. Of the few people who viewed these written "works-in-progress" while he lived, apparently none corrected his grammatical habits. Consistently throughout he adds "e" with the "ing" suffix, dots each "g" as if it were "j", abbreviates "et cetera" as "ect." and spells "escape" with "ex." But what is a misplaced comma amidst the prophecies of "Terra Revolution and Venus"? Only a fool would complain of incidentals while interpreting such poetry.

The writings in this book expand our understanding of Hendrix. Familiar lyrics take on added and altered meanings, while previously unknown songs tease us with unheard melodies. But it is impossible to accurately date most of these pieces. They span the last four years of Jimi's life: from 1967 to 1970 up until his very last poem, composed just hours before death.

From documented dates of known recording sessions for songs included in this book, and from hotel stationery cross-referenced with Jimi's tour schedule, we've been able to arrange a basic chronology for the writings. But within this progression we've elected to insert several pieces according to a parallel time-line of themes, grouping writings together based on related internal images. For example, the first song in the book, "Mr. and Miss Carriage," is written on Red Carpet Inn stationery. Although we know that Jimi stayed at the Red Carpet Inn when he played in Charlotte, North Carolina, on May 9, 1969, it is well known that he often carried hotel stationery in his flight bag for several weeks or months before he wrote on it. And even though "Mr. and Miss Carriage" exists on paper *most likely* used during 1969, we can't know whether or not Jimi had *other* drafts of these lyrics dating from years earlier. With such potential pitfalls regarding dates for most of the writings, we should explain how and why we arrived at the ordering of the writings in this book.

Our chronology starts with the themes of Jimi's early years, beginning with his prebirth view from the womb. "Mr. and Miss Carriage" was eventually rewritten and christened "Belly Button Window," for its debut as the closer for Jimi's *Cry of Love* album, which ironically was the first posthumous Hendrix release. "I wrote a song on abortion," he said in 1969.

> They should legalize abortion! See, evolution is changing the brain, so quite naturally you're gonna have hang-ups of thought, but still the whole past is going towards a higher-way of thinking, towards a *clearer* way of thinking. But there are still some hard-heads that . . . don't give theirselves a chance to develop in the brain, or let their souls develop, or the emotions. . . . This *is* a modern age and they do have pills for this. But just make sure those *pills* are proper because some of those pills make people sick. . . . And some of these girls get very sick trying *not* to have babies. And who says that it's *written* that . . . it's a sin to, what-they-call, kill off a "child"? A child isn't a *child* until it comes out into the air. I don't think so. They have to think in a higher range of thinking. A lot of young people are. They're gonna get it together.

The next writing is a one-page outline for a song titled "War Child," placed here to commemorate Jimi's birth on November 27, 1942, during the height of World War II. "War Child" is possibly a sketch for the song Jimi debuted at the June 1969 Newport Pop Festival, where he sang the refrain "There's a war going on, child." This tune may be a forerunner of "Machine Gun," the antiwar anthem Jimi debuted two months later.

"Hospital Snore" most likely dates from 1969 or later, because scribbled out at the page top in someone else's hand (not shown) is the note, "Call Roland Kirk—about Jimi's record." Jimi and Roland Kirk jammed together in early 1969. And Hendrix is known to have visited hospitals several times during his career. But "Hospital Snore" is placed early in our chronology to commemorate his very earliest memory:

> I must have been in the hospital sick about something. I remember a nurse putting a diaper on me and almost sticking me. She

took me out of this crib and held me up to the window, and she was showing me something up against the sky. It was fireworks, it must have been the Fourth of July. That nurse turned me on, high on penicillin she probably gave me. I was looking up and the sky was just . . . SsschuussSchush! Our first trip there.

While "Our Lovely Home" and "Clara Crenshaw" are not datable, they both convey childlike images easily associated with Jimi's boyhood.

"Different States of America" is written on the back of Michael Jeffery Management stationery, which dates from sometime after mid-1968 when Jeffery bought out his partner, Chas Chandler's, interest in The Jimi Hendrix Experience. "Different States" is placed here to mark Jimi's maturing as a citizen who thought deeply about what it means to be American. By the same stroke, "I See Arms and Hands" reflects his multicultural heritage. It isn't difficult to imagine an army-bound Jimi writing of "our home in our hearts" which "we must protect."

"Would it burn me if I touch the sun" is a line from "Love Or Confusion," lyrics of which appear on London's Hyde Park Towers stationery. Jimi has arrived in England. "Love Or Confusion" was among the early original compositions recorded by The Jimi Hendrix Experience after they'd released their breakthrough hit, "Hey Joe." "They'd picked out 'Love Or Confusion' to be our next single," Jimi told the press, "but I had this thing on my mind about walking on the sea. Then I wrote 'Purple Haze.' "

With his new British fame, Jimi incurred epithets of "Mau Mau" and "Wild Man of Borneo" from London tabloids, thus "Sticks and Stones" offers a belated reply. The title track of his first album, *Are You Experienced?*, contains the line "trumpets and violins/I can hear in the distance . . .", however music for the separate poem titled "Trumpets and Violins, Violins" remains unheard.

Around the time of his band's American debut at the Monterey Pop Festival in June 1967, Jimi cowrote a long poem with Nancy Rainer titled "The World Eats," from which appears the excerpt "Now the Street Lights." The next three writings, "Please Help Me," "A Cry From One Soul to Its Mate," and "Bold as Love," also come from the Summer of Love. From August 9–13 Jimi stayed at the Shoreham Hotel in Washington, D.C., while the Experience were booked at the Ambassador Theater. On Shoreham stationery survives lyrics for the title track of his next album, *Axis: Bold as Love*. *Axis* is also represented by lyrics for its opening song, "Up from the Skies."

"My Friend" was recorded on March 13, 1968. The lyrics refer to Jimi's January 4 one-nighter in a "Scandinavian jail" for trashing his hotel room in Sweden. He also mentions Harlem and L.A., places he had recently visited while on tour. A week after recording "My Friend," Jimi wrote in his daily diary about meeting Joni Mitchell in Ottawa. Following his March 22 entry, he maintained the diary only occasionally, however, on the way to Rochester on March 20 he refers to "our plans for a movie." It is this reference which prompted our placement of the *Moon Dust* screenplay, page two of which describes "a little innocent girl watching 3 guys playing music (Mitch, Noel and me)."

There follow two pieces representing the 1968 *Electric Ladyland* album: "Long Hot Summer Night" and "1983."

A lot of songs are fantasy type songs, so people think you don't know what you're talking about at all, but it all depends on what the track before and after might have been. Like you might tell them something kinda hard but you don't want to be a completely hard character in their minds and be known for all that, 'cause there's other sides of you and sometimes they leak on to the records too. That's when the fantasy songs come in. Like for instance "1983"—that's something to keep your mind off what's happening today, but not necessarily completely hiding away from it like some people might do with certain drugs and so forth.

In August 1967 the Experience were filmed at the Rudolf Valentino mansion in Los Angeles. There they spent time inside a room covered from floor to ceiling with mirrors. A year later Jimi was back in L.A. for an extended stay during which he began recording early versions of "Room Full of Mirrors." In observance of this L.A. connection, we've placed next the Beverly Rodeo stationery pages containing "Please Mr. Lover Man," with its "mirror, mirror on the wall" image. This poem's line, "her kiss is a cup of sunshine" leads effectively into the next piece, "Kiss the Sunshine."

During the winter of 1969, plans were drawn up for the construction of Jimi's recording studio. An April 17 note from Jimi preserves several names being considered for the project, before an April 22 memo from Jim Marron introduces the title "Electric Lady, Inc."

"Thank You God" is scrawled on stained butcher paper and contains lyrics first heard during Jimi's version of "Voodoo Child (Slight Return)" from the April 26, 1969, Forum concert in L.A. Two weeks later he was back on the East Coast for a gig in Charlotte, North Carolina. It is from here that the Red Carpet Inn stationery, containing "Electric Stagehand" as well as "Mr. and Miss Carriage," originates.

On May 18 Jimi played in Madison Square Garden, another "Roman Coliseum," as he called such arenas when he ad-libbed lyric asides during concerts on that massive spring tour. Except for two dates in late June, the tour ended at Waikiki on June 1. A week later Jimi reflected his island vacation with the lushly imaged "Valleys of Neptune." If he'd felt like a modern gladiator while on tour, at least there was peace in the valley: "I feel the ocean swaying me/washing away all my pains/See where I used to be wounded/remember the scar? Now you can't see a thing . . ."

"Ball and Chain For Sale" is dated July 19, 1969, the day before Neil Armstrong became the first man to walk on the moon. The Experience had disbanded permanently three weeks earlier and Jimi took a trip to Morocco. When he returned he settled into a rented house near Woodstock to rehearse a new group. But when staying in New York, his on-going "homebases" were often Hotel Elysée and Hotel Navarro. Writings on stationery from these hotels are impossible to date, except for the few pages already dated by Jimi himself, like "Ball and Chain For Sale."

Placed at the time of the moon landing, in the season of hurricanes, "As I Gaze Into My Crystal Ball," on "fly the friendly skies" stationery, is rife with lunar/space references: *between Earth and the moon, soaring through space, landed on Mars, desert Earth, spinning slave pebble earth, UFOs, vapor trails, platforms of launching pads, tun-*

nels through the sky, axis turns, last rocket up, the moon's meadows. Within 1969's space-age context, "Crystal Ball" reads like a metaphor for the moon. Could Diana, with her "tear" and "mud brothers," refer to the 1955 hurricane? In "Electric Stagehand" Jimi wrote of the "World Hurricane," and during his concert at Woodstock on the morning of August 18, the most powerful storm ever recorded plowed through the South. Hurricane Camille hit Mississippi's Delta, ripping up the birthplace of the Blues, while Jimi tore apart the National Anthem for "500,000 Halos," at Woodstock. It was as if a voodoo priest had raised valleys of Neptune to kiss the sky for peace in Mississippi.

"Meet Me in the Country" commemorates Jimi's rural retreat near Woodstock that summer. When he played the festival he introduced his new band as Gypsy Sun & Rainbows. They arrived on stage "right before the morning's came to Earth."

Although the music for "Sippin' Time, Sippin' Wine" remains unknown, we do know that "I'm Traveling a Speed" became the lyrics for "Message to Love," an early title of which is likely seen as "Power of God . . . Love to Devon" on Jimi's "Songs to Try" list. This song, along with "Come on Down," were part of A Band Of Gypsys' repertoire in late 1969. A Band Of Gypsys was rock's first black power trio.

As the BOG progressed, Jimi composed a suite of songs under the title of "Black Gold." These songs were considered for possible multimedia treatment. The closest he came to describing this project to the press is believed to be in a February 4, 1970 interview with John Burk for *Rolling Stone*.

I just try to have some time to myself so I can really write some things, 'cause I want to do more writing. Mostly it's cartoon material; make up this one cat who's funny, who goes through these strange scenes. It's all funny, I guess. You put it to music, just like how you can put blues into music. I want to get into what you'd probably call "pieces," behind each other to make movements. I've been writing some of those. You listen to it and you get such funny flashbacks (laughs). The music is going along with the story. Just like "Foxy Lady." The music and the words go together.

One of the groundbreaking features of this book is our partial reconstruction of lyrics for the suite of songs known as "Black Gold." Jimi sketched out these songs on acoustic guitar in a continuous stream for his portable recorder. The suite includes: "November Morning," "Drifting," "Captain 1201," "Loco Commotion," "Here Comes Black Gold," "Steppingstone," "Little Red Velvet Room," "The Jungle Is Waiting," "Send My Love to Joan of Arc," "God Bless the Day," "Machine Gun," "Black Gold" (refrain), "Trash Man," "Astro Man," and "I've Got a Place to Go."

In 1967 Jimi said, "This one song I wrote, 'Eyes and Imagination,' that's the name of it, is about fourteen minutes long. But every sentence or every two sentences tell a completely different story. It's nothing but imagination. It starts off with this baby crying, a brand new baby has been born, and then you hear these bullets, you know (laughs), in the background. It goes on in about four major movements, but it always goes back to this one little theme, it must have that one little theme through it." It makes sense that the "one little theme" repeated throughout this mysterious piece called "Eyes and Imagination" may be "the wink of an eye." The miscellaneous page we've included at the end of the "Black Gold" poem is placed here because it relates to the last line of "Black Gold": "within the wink of an eye." It is this page which conforms to Jimi's "new born baby crying/bullets" theme: "with the wink of an eye, a new born baby cries, and a hundred soldiers die, with the wink of an eye." It is also poignant how Jimi's own life conforms to the metaphor; he was born at the height of the Second World War with "these bullets in the background" and several times throughout his writings he incorporates the "wink of an eye" image, including, within the very last lines he ever wrote, which are seen for the first time in script form at the end of this book, "it always goes back to this one little theme."

"May I Whisper in Your Ear" is placed near the end of the "Black Gold" chronology because of its association with the lyrics for "Trash Man."

During his spring 1970 trip, Jimi stayed at the Londonderry Hotel. It is the only time he is known to have stayed there except for a couple of nights prior to the Isle of Wight Festival in August. For this reason, "Pass It On," "One Kiss of Your Eyes" and "Moonlife in Spiral Light" appear here in the book. "The Terra Revolution and

Venus" follows because the notepad it was written on is the same paper used for "Send My Love to Joan of Arc."

"Midnight Lightning" and "In From the Storm" are two atmospheric disturbance pieces which were among the last three songs (along with "Dolly Dagger") added to Jimi's concert set in the summer of '70. "In From the Storm" (as well as "Dolly Dagger") was debuted during the July 30 concert on Maui, where Jimi signed his host's guest book as a member of the Antahkarana production staff there to film the show.

"Nightbird Flying" is another song from that summer. It is placed here to allow Jimi's "wrap me up in your wings" earthy "Nightbird" to "spread her wings high over me" as "Angel." "Angel" was a tune he'd been refining for several years. The song was finally heard on the *Cry of Love* LP after his death. "Angel" appears here in the book for its theme of anticipated redemption. Then, in "Forget of My Name," we are directed to his nonpersonal identity, "the waves of my interpreture," a metaphysical vehicle for some addressing inhabitance—"my belief, which is God." At the "staircase of birth" we find Jimi back "up here in this womb," looking out of a "Belly Button Window," ready to "go back to Spiritland" until his next incarnation.

With his final tour over on September 6, Jimi returned to London and booked into the Cumberland Hotel. This was the only time he is known to have stayed there. On Cumberland stationery he sketched a series of seemingly unrelated verses and brought the drafts with him to the Samarkand Hotel, where he stayed with Monika Dannemann on September 15. Two nights later, after attending a party until early in the morning, Jimi returned to the Samarkand with Monika and wrote "The Story of Life" before they went to bed. He never woke up.

For their insights regarding Jimi's whereabouts, which helped shape the chronology of this book, I thank Tony Brown, Alan Douglas, Kathy Etchingham, Bill Nitopi, and Noel Redding.

Compiled from dozens of different interviews, what follows is a collection of Jimi's thoughts and attitudes about his ways of writing:

You don't plan songwriting. You don't get in a certain groove to write a song, you dig? You can get inspiration for a song any time, because music is just what you feel. Sometimes you see things in different ways than other people could see it, so then you write it in a song. It could represent anything. We go to clubs a lot and go all around in taxis and you happen to see a lot of things. You see everything, experience everything as you live. Even if you're living in a little room, you see a lot of things if you have imagination.

A lot of times you get an idea from something you might have seen, and then you can write it down the way it *really* happened, or you can write it down the way you might have *wanted* it to happen, or the way it *could* have happened. The songs just come. I like to explore whatever happens to them, that's enough. You go into different moods and when you write, your moods come through. That's the only way I can explain myself thoroughly, is through songs.

I've written about 100 songs, but they're all over the place; like in hotel rooms in the States where I didn't pay the rent. In fact, I'd like to go back and pay all the back rent I owe just so I can get those songs back! A lot of times I write a lot of words all over the place, anywhere: on matchboxes, or on napkins. And then sometimes the music comes across to me just when I'm sitting around doing nothing, and the music makes me think of a few words I might have written, so I go back to those few words, if I can find them, and just get it together.

I'm very inconsistent, it all depends on how I feel. Sometimes I write in a rush, but the things I'm writing now take a little longer to say. Most of them that I do, I come up with the music, then I could put the words so much easier that fit the type of music that it makes me think of. And then other times when you get nice words together, you have to think of the music that could fit it. Sometimes it all happens at the same time. All depends on what you might want to say, different moods you might be in. There's no certain patterns I go by.

But I stay in bed most of the time, or go to the park or somewhere. That's where I write some of my best songs, in bed, just laying there. Sometimes you might be by yourself writing something and you come across some words and you just lay back and dig the words and see how that makes you feel. And you might take it to practice or rehearsal or something like that and get together with it there with music, see how the music feels. Or sometimes you might be jammin' or something, and you keep runnin' across that. Then you start shouting out anything that comes to your mind, whatever the music turns you on to. If it's heavy music, you start singin' things.

Songs are like a personal diary. Most of the songs, like "Purple Haze" and "The Wind Cries Mary," were about ten pages long, but we're restricted to a certain time limit so I had to break them all down. Once I'd broken the songs down I didn't know whether they were going to be understood or not. Maybe some of the meanings got lost by breaking them down, which I never do any more, it's such a drag. If you write an abstract song, for instance, with slightly abstract words that don't go exactly like "I love you, will you screw me tonight?" it doesn't go exactly like that, it might go "I felt the ceiling fall under me" and all this mess, you know, then you can make the *sound* happen. In studios now you can actually emphasize certain words that you want to get across. Instead of saying, "Will you make love to me tonight?" all of a sudden there's this big crash!

What I like to do is write a lot of mythical scenes, like the history of the wars on Neptune and all this mess, and the reason why the rings are there. See, like how they've got the Greek gods and all that mythology, well you can have your *own* mythology scene, or write fiction, *complete* fiction though. I mean, anybody can say, "I was walkin' down the street and I seen a elephant floatin' through the sky." Well, it has no meaning at all, there's nothing to imagine, except there's this elephant there, and if you don't watch out you might break your neck [laughs]. But the way I write things, I just write with a clash between reality and fantasy mostly. You have to use fantasy in order to show different sides of reality, just how it can bend. I want to write mythology stories set to music, based on a planetary thing and my imagination in general. Maybe I'm going to write a big thing, maybe not. I'd have to look around and see what's around the house.

There's so many songs I wrote that we haven't done yet,

that we'll probably never do. It's because there's a lot of things around here that's a really bad scene—we must be "Elvis Presleys" and "rock 'n' rolls" and "Troggs," we must be *that* (laughs). And there'll be no smoking in the gas chamber (laughs). Every time we come into town everybody always looks towards us for some kind of answer to what's happening to them. Which is a good feeling, but it's very hard. So therefore I have to live the *life;* I have to witness all these bad scenes, and all these good scenes so then I can say, "Well, what *I* found out . . ." you know, instead of just reading books. Anybody can protest but hardly anybody tries to give a decent type of solution, at least a meantime solution. So therefore I'm gonna get all these words together in nice heavy songs, very straightforward songs, and just sock it to 'em—properly.

—MICHAEL FAIRCHILD

JIMI HENDRIX
CHEROKEE MIST

THE LOST WRITINGS

Seattle, February 12, 1968

(Douglas Kent Hall)

Say Hello to my
Mother and Father.....
the Earth and Space

1

Mr. and Miss Carraige

Red Carpet Inn

TELEPHONE 377-5911 Area Code 704
TWX 704 525 2420

1615 E. MOREHEAD ST. / CHARLOTTE, N. C. 28202

Blue beat on chorus verse will be sung with parade beat

1. well I'm up here in this womb, looking all around --- I look at my belly button window. and I see nothing but frowns ★ And I think they... don't want me... around.

2. well what's all this fuss, what seems to be the sham... I mean damn, if they don't want me, hell I'll go back to Spirit land... And even take me a longer rest before coming down this chute again ... Man I remember the last time ... they was still arguing about mo-then-
★ And if you don't... want me now...
please make up your mind... where and when —
Break → Because I AINT comeing THIS WAY TOO MUCH
MUCH MORE AGAIN OH NO —>

3. what is that, is that a doctor, Hey bro' watch out for that thing — You act like my potential mixed up
MaMa is carrying an orangutang —
You say how do I know what a monkey is man we all been here before... so as soon as you people stop pokeing me... I'll be obliged if you close that door ... ★ And make up your mind.... give or take... you only got... 200 days AND THEN (over)

I'm comeing out Daddy regardless of love or hate — I'm gonna sit up in your Bed and GRIN IN YOUR FACE — AND THEN I'm no EAT UP ALL YOUR CHOCOLATES AND SAY "I HOPE I'M NOT LATE"

notes: Keep 1st verse and 2nd verse
1st verse for chorus repeat
repeat "Belly Button window" in verse and also 2nd chorus
repeat after solo —
last verse about pills, ills
chills, thrills, spills

2

"Gypsy Eyes" (Illustration by Thomas Yeates)

well you know people get all those pills for chills, ills
and thrills and then when it comes to
us babies, you don't know what you feel
is real... So if you want abortion by all means
please go head just Because you know
So you won't mess me up with some It ain't kool to bring me up with no o bread

especially when that world outside is
So cold Hateful and dead
So legalize, if you're wise
for me to lay back
or for to rise
Ot else, find something else
for you'all to do

Red Carpet Inn

War Child

(Note:) to go on war side of L.P.   working key of F#

INDIAN APRO BASS out; for intro   E   HIGH F#

1. Well I'm a... — war child...   Boom ect ∞   E

BASS and glitter repeat 9 beat for every note change

Boom 1
Boom 2
Boom 3
Boom 4
Boom 5
Boom 6
Boom 7
Boom 8
Boom 2

U or Group Repeat 3 times with notes of
→ F
war child is ... @Ab   A Ab A Ab Going crazy.

" " 2
" " 3
" " 4
" " 5
" " 6
ect... ect...

then Guitar. plane sands and whistles from high pitch
Diveing to Low pitch like Bombs.
when they hit ... 2nd line prepares and
then Start in tempo beat again for whole
Repeat of every thing except vocals and
Bombs for 2nd line.

2.

---

the Hospital's snore
the Moter cycles roar
and the cops are whipping
your head more and more

No help for the Helpless
No more for the poor

Our Lovely Home.

They're ~~out in the sun~~ *out in the sun* throwing Snowballs
at my window
Birds and airplanes flyin through
the halls - A shoe full of holes is
laughing ~~at~~ the wallpaper people
Besides all that, aint too much
happenin at all -

All the free Bees ~~tryin to steal~~ tryin to steal
honey from our flowers - Cats ~~peeing~~ *peppermint*
and dogs raining down on the ~~roof~~ roof
purple Buffalos dancing in the *spring*
~~and~~
~~the Swimming Pool~~ Besides all that, everything
is KOOL

~~(scribbled out lines)~~

Our neighbours are so sweet, they
never complain *cos* on the left ~~there~~
~~lives~~ lives Kinky Capt. Curry - and
on the right ~~lives~~ lives inky Dandy Jane
and I think the whole blocks insane)

Skinny Girls slidding down the
banisters and in the ~~courtyard~~
~~Screaming~~ yard screaming up
with stoned freaks
Im sitting on a bottom ~~stair~~ slipping on a ½cup of soap
~~(House)~~ ~~too~~ and I whisper to you
please pass the ~~cheese~~ cheese

Chellophane and kryptinte critics
Chopping on ~~Curtis's~~ petrified Tree
and they're ax blades breakin tiny
Pieces - they ~~take~~ take revenge)
by ~~gang~~ gangin' up on a flea
who ... ~~is blind~~ is minding his
business walking ~~into~~ to our house
and he comes running in with a
~~bruise~~ charlie horse and busted lip

5

1. Poor Miss Clara Crenshaw
2. died this morning God
3. rest her little wrinkled bones
4. it seems by looking at the
5. way the window pane (shattered)
6. that she had a very bad
7. cold and, well... I know
8. you've seen the size of her
9. nose I mean It's... er ah,
10. well anyway, I heard tell
11. that she rolled away from
12. her shadow of a husband's
13. advances, the wretched devil)
14. any how, she rolled over, caught
15. her nose in her ear, sneezed
16. and blew her brains out
17.
18.
19.
20.

Negative Nellie episode:

Chapt. 15.

look at 'em up there preaching

Knowing all the time

they're steady reaching~

Squeezing you away from

Your pennies nickels and dimes

rideing the robe of Jesus...

and who ever else that

feeds us, Hollering "Any friend of Batman's

is a friend of mine...

any time...

for a dime

6

we are diffrent
States of America.
we are not United.
Some of us wish to be.
~~the~~ But only in
Times of war ~~of and~~
or Love —
But those are bare
2 reasons - Americans
they are specific —
Unity represents the
need of strength extra,
for on comeings, opposition
ATTACK — WE are
foolish to think of attack
unless we have the

the same inner
*intentions —
In the early morning
let us scratch
The word United —
for Reason of unnessarly
~~&~~ Closeness explanation to Love.
of on comeing Games
of war ... need added
strength ect —

We are diffrent
~~states~~ of America
United never need
to be said or thought
of when bringing
or giveing or Shareing
Love — But we know we
are ... A part of ___!

Michael Jipp
27 East 5 1/2 Street
New York New York 10019
N.Y. U.S.A.

Jolly Roger Club, Nashville, Tennessee, 1964 (David Pearcy Collection)

Hotel Elysée

I See arms and hands
and tear stained faces...
Reaching up but not quite
touching the promise land —
I hear pleas and prayers
and desperate graces —
Saying Oh Lord, please
give us a helping hand —
there's going to be a
war ..... we must protect
our homes —

Hotel Elysée

we won't wait for
too much longer — We must
protect our home ... Yes
Yes Our home in our hearts.
Well I See black and
white and red and yellow
even green — getting together
And their weapons are
Shining clean — But I'm
not talking about swords, knives
and guns — I'm talking about
the power of God from the new
Riseing Sun

Give me some room to breathe.
I don't want to nessecerily Breathe
on you (gear)

Street cleaner + fireman [Drum solo]
haveein' a hard time washing
me off street
my Mother and the laundry
haveen' a hard time keeping
me with clean sheets
Now I aint doing so bad
~~Explain~~ haveing you could
make me feel so bad
but her must (attune) Give me some
room too. I dont always went to see you
Give me some room to think
I dont want to neccessarly think
about you. Eventhough I may
Just steal a drink, the
Cops dont have to come to you too
No telling what we could do + you can
Bring your sister too But (give idea)
Give me room after while
I ~~dont~~ / dount want for you to cop my style

Guitar Sdo. I see only one window
When there two Before. Tree only
3 walls when I know these
Should be 4   2nd Lord is what happen to the door
look
Give me some room to be me
I dont want to always have to be you

Drum Break
King ~~Kong~~ and his
Sisters they train. hard just to cut no
doin. The funeral of my silk
Jacket. It's trying (2nd) just to make
me frown

And even thorzgh I tripped on
you. there was nothing else
for us to do
Please Give me some room
to get straight I dont always want to
get straight with you

9

IV.

How did Sadness, enter my
life, fate asks....
I reply without a word or
sound — one slip of the
tongue......... I slip deeper
into everlasting sorrow)))))))☺

Broken Hearted am I... My pride
attempts to comfort me — But
love dampens my eyes to where
I can't see — Love .... Hurt love
takes over and cries out—

This pain, I cannot
Bear : I beg Mercy
in name of forgiveness
....

(Fast, slight spanish)
(Here comes the sun)
Chords (accented)

E   B   F#
Look at the Sun rise —
D   A   E
Here comes the Sun rise
Repeat Twice —

Shining   Then Break with Guitar and
in my   Bells — Guitar 1st E string
life   ring open as B and G strings
          Playing slight oriental pattern
          Together
                B string notes start on 7th fret
          with G string on 6th ...
Numbers   like So: 8 7 123 10 123 12 ...
represent   Then 5 123 7 123 10
Beat   Repeat with low Click
                of Bass and slide Slide
                Guitar coming from down
          Notes to up —
          Then vocal and at same Time,
          Guitar hitting G chord, and Bass
          string and Bass guitar hitting
          A ... then syncopate chords of B min,
          C#m, D, up to G.... then to B — over

Key of
F#

10

New Century Hall, Manchester, England, January 7, 1967. Harry Goodwin/Starfile

is that the stars in the sky or is it rain coming
down
would it burn me if I touch the sun, so big
so round —
must there always be these colors, without names
without sound
. would I be lying if I said you're the one

**Saville Theatre, London,
June 4, 1967**
(Bill Nitopi Collection)

MAY THIS BE
LOVE OR JUST
CONFUSION BORN OUT OF
FRUSTRATION WRACKED
FEELINGS OF NOT
BEING
MAKE TRUE   ABLE TO
LOVE TO   PHYSICAL
              THE
UNIVERSAL GYPSIE Queen
OF TRUE, FREE EXPRESSED MUSIC.
MY DARLING GUITAR... PLEASE
REST IN PEACE. AMEN

Purple Haze
~ Jesus Saves

Purple Haze...Bey ond insane
Is it pleasure or is it
pain ~
Dawn On the ~~see~~ ~~eted~~ ceiling
looking up at the
~~Bed~~... See my Body painted
Blue and red ~

I see fetus's unborns
~~Why is everybody~~
pointing at the Time ~~~
Rush through space...
my Hair is Blowing in thier minds
~~forgetting~~ through the Hazes
I see 1,000 crosses
Scratched in the ~~~

Now the street lights
~~have~~ been turned on and
they shine more light than
was ~~formely~~ formely allowed
by way of restlessness of the
kik of progress ~~~ or deepress...
So now I shall die or
strike gold. or blow a fuse
and say forth to you......

sticks and stones can't
Break my soul
But words; They seem to
ometimes Warm me ~
Maloye it's because
I'm forever hungry ~
... for the throth
of love

Jimi with best friend Brian Jones at Monterey Pop Festival, June 18, 1967

(Copyright © 1992 Paul Kagan)

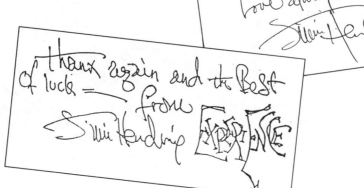

Hollywood Bowl, August 18, 1967 *(Copyright © 1993 Flower Children Ltd/Chuck Boyd)*

Fifth Dimension Club, Ann Arbor, Michigan, August 15, 1967 *(Wilson Lindsey)*

Please Help Me —

ONLY FOR A WHILE ...
But please
Help me —

Fifth Dimension Club, Ann Arbor, Michigan, August 15, 1967
(Wilson Lindsey)

a cry from one soul to it's mate:

..... "Please ..... please help me. they're
Trying to take me away ...
for .... for a crime That
I just can't help ... A crime they
Say I committed to make people happy
Sad, indefferent, deaf, climax, cry,
laugh, life, intertaintment ..."forget
your life and fancy, young slave
You belong to us , Ha Ha Ha"....
Please Gold & Rose , ... please
help me ......"!
And he knows That fate is a jealous, Queen Whore
of lives
signed:
Beyond Love — But I will feel and we
Both understand

The SHOREHAM
Hotel and Motor Inn
CONNECTICUT AVENUE AT CALVERT STREET
Washington 8, D.C.

Anger Smiles, standing in Shiny Mettalic
purple armour - Queen Jealousy &
Envy waits behind him - Her fire
green gown laughs at the grassy ground
Blue are the life-giveing waters,
close to them they understand
takeing for Granted, they Quitley
under stand - once-happy Torqouise Armys
lays opposite ready, But wondering
why the fight is on

The SHOREHAM
Hotel and Motor Inn
CONNECTICUT AVENUE AT CALVERT STREET
Washington 8, D.C.

Yellow in this case is not so mellow
in fact, I'm Trying to say, its
frightened like me,
But ALL OF THESE is still out there
love to a rainbow

And all of these emotions of mine
keeps holding me from
love to you putting my life
my life to you Giveing my life to
You
Rainbow

Anger the Smiles, stood towering, in Shiny
Mettalic purple armour - Queen Jealousy
Envy waits behind him - her fire green
gown legs sners at the grassy ground
Blue are the life-giveing waters
Takeing for granted, they Quietly understand.
once-happy Torqouise Armys ley oppisite ready
But wondering why the fight is on
But their all bold as love.... Just ask the AXIS,
Red symbol, clash
words f So confident. he flashes
Trophies of war and
Ribbons of pleasure euphoria
Orange is Young, full of dancing
to But very UN at first
so round steady for the first
YELLOW, in this case), not so mellow,
IN FACT I'm Trying to say its
frightened like me - cant
understand BUT IN THE converstation
BOUT IMAGE

17

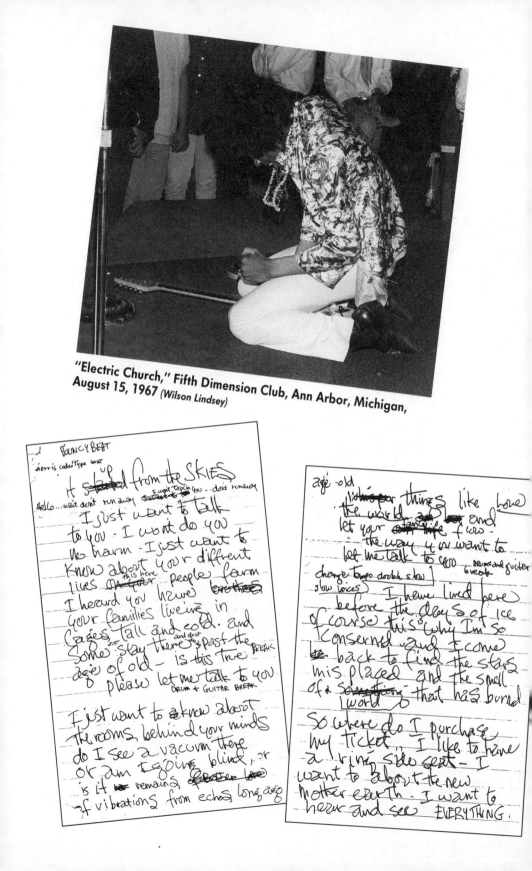

"Electric Church," Fifth Dimension Club, Ann Arbor, Michigan, August 15, 1967 *(Wilson Lindsey)*

"Out of the shadows . . ." Fillmore East, New York City, May 10, 1968 *(Copyright © 1993 Elliot Landy)*

Seattle, February 12, 1968 *(Douglas Kent Hall)*

Boston Garden, November 16, 1968 *(Copyright © 1993 Leonard Eisenberg)*

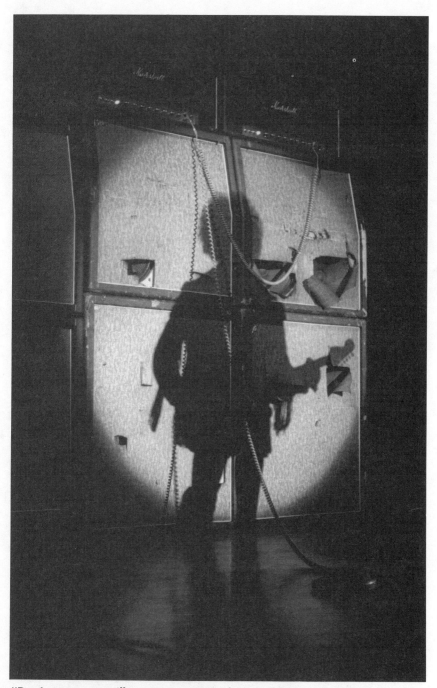

"Don't expect me, till you see me." Woolsey Hall, Yale University, New Haven, Connecticut, November 17, 1968 *(Joe Sia)*

Washington Hilton Hotel, March 10, 1968 (John Gossage)

**Fillmore West,
San Francisco,
February 2, 1968**
(George Feist)

"And into the light," Harlem, New York City, September 5, 1969
(Jim Cummins/Starfile)

"See my baby
Coming across the Sun
Coming across the Sun
Paradise in love has just begun."
Civic Auditorium, Bakersfield, California, October 26, 1968

Civic Auditorium, Bakersfield, California, October 26, 1968
(Copyright © 1970 Larry Hulst/Michael Ochs Archives/Venice, California)

Seattle, February 12, 1968 *(Douglas Kent Hall)*

26

Pan-Am press conference,
New York City,
January 31, 1968
(Don Paulsen)

TITLE:

" if found lost... please return to Body"
         or West coast Seattle Boy

1. Hey My feet's on fire, Head in the air
Loveing, life and flowing free is
my only care. (music Break)

I feel Fine, Don't mind dying (cause)
WHEN I do, there's no harm in crying
I'm just a west coast Seattle Boy—

2. Well I ride me a stage coach
up to your rave porch
You Better have some Ocean
(cause) I'm carrying me a torch

HOTEL Navarro
ON-THE-PARK
112 central park south, new york, n.y. 10019
212 circle 7-7900
Cable NAVARROTEL

San Francisco, February 2, 1968 *(Baron Wolman)*

Shrine Auditorium, Los Angeles, February 10, 1968 (Bill Kerby)

Well I'm rideing through L.A.
on a bycicklye built for fools
I seen one of my old buddies, he
say you don't look the way you used to do
I said well some people look like a
coin box- He said look like you aint got
no coins to spare - I just picked
up my pride from under neath the pay
phone and collected
combed his ~~Brenda~~ out of my hair
And sometimes it's not so easie
especially when you have a friend
that talks to you looks like you feel like you
and you look and talk like him
I just got out of a scandinavian
Jail and Now I'm on my way to
you. I look in the mirror to make
sure that my friends with me here too
and you know I don't drink coffee
so you feel my cup full of sand. But
The frozen tea leafs at the bottom
and the lipstick smear around the
broken edge, and my coat that youlet
your dog lay by the fire on

Well I'm wandering through Harlem
before my back bone and
A stage coach full of feathers and
foot prints pulls up to my soap box
door
A lady with a pearl handled neckTie
Tied to the drivers fence - breathed out
burbon and coke possessed words
Havent I seen you somewhere in hell
or what if just zen accident.
Before I could ask was it the east
of west side, My feet they howled in pain
the wheels of her bandwagon dug
very deep, But not as deep as in my
mind as the rain. As they pulled away
I could see her words stagger
and fall on my muddy tent
I picked them up, brushed them off, to see
what they said. Come round to my
room with the in the middle
and writeing along 2 presidents

Seattle, February 12, 1968 *(Douglas Kent Hall)*

UCLA Auditorium, February 13, 1968 (Copyright © 1993 Flower Children Ltd/Chuck Boyd)

MARCH 19

Arrived in Ottawa — Beautiful dinner... Strange people... Beautiful dinner hel... talked with Joni Mitchell on the phone — I think I'll record her tonight with my excellent tape recorder (knock on wood) Hmmm... cant find any wood — everythings plastic. Beautiful views. Sound on first show Good on 2nd. Marveloes. went down to the little club to see Good recording. fantastic girl with heaven words we all got to Joni — Ok. millions of girls... listen to tapes and smoked dope! party...

MARCH 20

We left Ottawa City today. I kissed Joni Goodbye. slept in the car and the Stoped at a highway diner. I mean a Real one. like in the movies. Mitch and I discuss air plans for movie. Slight disagreement here and there but it will be soon straighten out. Nothing happened in Rochester Tonight. Went to a very bad bad a Bad Tasteing restrant. Thugs follow us. they probebly was scared. couldnt figure us out. the with my Indian hat and Mexican moustach. Mitch with his fairy tale Jacket and Noel with his leapeard band hat and Glasses and hair And accent... G'nite all.

MARCH 21

Today we play Rochester NY. really a strange town ..... oh well ... Two girls came up to my room by the names of Heidi and Barbra — Real groovy people. we played one show Tonight — very bad p.a. Bad Hall. patient people but I kind of lost my Temper with everything in general. recorded show with Tape recorder. After Show we go to girls house with party material. Some all outside got beat up by the Hackers. stayed there over night in the Tiger room ok CONN.

MARCH 22

Today we're in Hartford Conn. I had a beautiful diary I kept while we were in Sweden — And of course I lost it. Hmmm I wonder what Catterina is doing now. I must call her soon, before she goes to Switzerland. She's the only thing I have to hold onto thats real. Better Call her soon. Beautiful room I have Bought more film, tape, etc... Just came back from Gig. Terrible. the people thought we were sweet. stage manager dropped the power right in the middle of our set. So I am depressed. Gonna get completely smashed. Hmmm let's see... where's that bottle.

31

characters,

1. ~~the Gypsis the~~ the power sand King.
2. his two friends
3. the super natural innocent girl
4. the super natural witch
5. the visual god.
6. party people
~~6~~7. the good guy.

Cerebrum   429
           BROOME st.
                   + crosby
   1 BK. EAST of
           BROADWAY

Story opens on same
countryside preverably
fields ,strange fields .
and a Gypsy arabian Timele
tent .... camera gets
closer ... goes inside of
tent , shows the (billing)
by showing diffrent
~~a plat~~ photos on walls
and little statoetts and
~~thing~~ ornaments inside
tent .... then music
explodes and the
west of the Titles are shown what interfers with
after titles and ~~credits~~.

32

shows a little ~~lost~~
innocent girl watching
3 guys playing music
(mitch, noel and me). She's
watching from behind
a rock or something.
film shows us straight
but through the girls
eyes, camera shows
the music as dragons,
then sugar things, then
evil things trying to be
born . all add to a hidden power ~~BUT~~

② all these things,
~~She~~ can only see, not even
the musicians.... only her.
She gets up and runs
away — ~~Here~~ and
~~us 3 have a few~~ we
~~words about~~ end the
song after noticing her
scampering off and we ~~both~~
~~laugh~~ laugh a little . a little
. rabbit
she is. HAHA
then we get serious ... discussing
the money problem and knowing
that we're good enough to
play for money - .... we start
. dinner. ~~me happy~~

we catch wild life, fry it viking style. we are talking about going into ④ Town, to jam somewhere to let people hear us, to be famous, we want. So a very exciting race scene into Town and our equipment (eric^may) driveing a freaked out truck full of our gear (fun scene) should be able to film some really good driveing scenes through windy roads ... Good exciting music ... finally arrive at a hot dog joint *

⑤ in town and meet Scott.

* ... a very special joint ...) the potential visual king. we make ~~~~ friends and he tells us places we could try to play and also trys to tell us or get a gig with us doing lights.] Scene at night — takes us to a club or some funky place and shows scene of innocent girl with beautiful colored girl across the Street from the club or at Club — And The colored girl saying "watch my darling" ... the beginning ..

is at hand "... or
something similar similar.
Then we play and
the music sways, ect....
ect... until until it gets
physical with the lights
and all. and so very
serious and soon people
are taking up on this
and then..... the power
fails and everything
is silent for about 20 seconds
Then... everybody laughs
and then flash to the girl and watch

and saying ---
"it is at hand and you
shall be Queen of Earth."
or something like this.

During Scene
where music HYPNOTIZES the
people, I went 2 scene where
a girl gets so completly
wrapped up in what's happening
that she tears
a shirt
off of
Stranger and without a word
they fall to the floor, making love.
This happens about 3 or 4
diffrent Times. with different people

almost to the point of (8)
no return, we will see)
a long beautiful brown
hand reach and turn
the power off (from the basement
or somewhere). Before this
we will show the witch
standing up to leave ... right
at the heat of the music —
any way ... the power goes off.
ect ..... everyone returns
to thier approx location
but still very dazed at the
impact. [the group gets the
gig . the next day the group
remodels the club to

Thier own taste . (9)
the innocent girl comes to visit
tells the player ....
.."Please be careful with your
power ... it could be dangrous
for the world" He says
"what power." and laughs very heavy
she runs away ... far away.
she runs all day she runs ....
music.. runs with her. taking her
diffrent scenes ... the sun sets.
the moon appears .... she feels better
she sings a song ... the moon
slips through the sky and dances with
her ...

the Sky dances ... She ⑩
is trippingly high ...so is
the Sky . the Sky makes
her feel much better because
she likes the player more and more
they (the sky and her) dance until she falls
(another day) asleep .
[More Scenes..... the group
s the biggest success since
air . ~~she~~ ~~makes it with the~~
~~Players~~ ~~he~~ ~~s~~ ~~her ...~~ ~~before~~
~~oing to work~~ ~~one night~~
)
Every where they play ...
the player starts to really want
the little girl . she is very beautiful
young and fresh. And she is
every where where they may be.

the player really digs the ⑪
witch too and makes love to her
several times ...the witch falls
hard on him she falls in real
love with him but doesn't want
him to hurt her innocent friend
and also doesn't want him
to have any one else.. He
travels the world , makes
love to the world's children .
they are happy ...Scenes
show the witch is burning...inside
the innocent girl falls in love
with him too.. He is sick in
the head .... He digs everything.
He ~~s~~ slightly loses himself in

the power and the pubic ⑫
~~eye~~ aroma of raw sex and
emotional music .. Music,
He is serious .. Sex, well,
who knows where his heads at.
Party Scene brings
a very strong emotional ~~scene~~ step.
in the film — —
the Timeless ~~scene~~ scene where a party
Speakeasy is raided flashes
of 30's and late 60's combine
to put today's police in a ~~silly~~ silly
but True out look on today's
old fashioned social laws.
Any way where was I ... oh yes.
a raid : Some people busted, Some

Killed, Some excape ..
we excape .. I excape with
the innocent girl we drive away
laugh and kiss, drive fast through
our high heads Through
roads, forests, worlds ...
finally to a deserted place
Set must be set very carefully
beauty and ugliness combined.
I want the girl very badly. I
show her I love her through
my music - She indicates ...
"what about my mother or
guardian"... I say "fuck her,
It's you and me" and I

38

have never been more (14)
Serious. we must capture
this scene to the fullest. we
stop... she runs off lay thing into the dark and I find
~~she her~~ on a beautiful cross
and we have no clothes.
Or something resembling
this... Mabye ~~two deer~~
a buck and a ~~deer~~ Doe then
change to a stallion and mare
and other ~~comcon~~ comparisions.
the innocent girl screams
" taste my world, my body,
my soul"... I am about to
go down on her and
make love to her. then
~~the~~ Witch in all the hall

of fire and Jealousy (15)
comes from nowhere
into shocking view.
the witch... the witch, the
witch is here - Not to
be said but to be <u>seen</u>
<u>cameras</u> Really do your
thing!.
the witch explains That Im am
fucked up in the head. I am
lost... she says ... I only want
her because she is diffrent,
she is young innocent, she
is helpless.... I argue
back. visual and sound shall

do thier up most to get
this across To the audience.
Can un dig what Im trying
to Say? . . . . He Hee He.
This is going to be ou Fa. site.
let's see now. . . hm. oh yes.
we have a battle, the witch
and I . . . But the witch
quite naturaly can't kill me
because I am insane almost.
and plus my power of Sound
come really and true key to life -
I kiss the young girl on the
Stomach and the witch
Screams a 1,000 voiced Scream

17

Throws off Some
kind of evil something on
me - But No! It doesn't quite
reach me Hatta.
My shield of Sound is too
powerful . . . Her evil
spell or spells bounces
ever so pitifully off and
out of the way - "witch, you
want me and her for the
Same as what you throw
in my face . . . I laugh
hysterically and throw
Sound waves on to her
which shakes This

Island of Battle to (18)
the end and I hurt her
So badly and the jolt is
So Strong that the innocent
girl, as She screams
~~you~~ you are man, I am women,
we belong, we are right
~~never mind her.~~ TAKE ME ....
She is wrong ect ... ect ...''
~~She~~ her cross crumbles
from the impact and she
Tumbles over the side
Of the cliff or a reasonable
facsimile of what She says
takes place ----
She ~~dies~~ dissappears is the

main point and the (19)
witch screams That I
have touched her, not her
body. I have fatally ~~wounded~~
her. I cry out "what have
I done? ~~(spoke)~~ Music at this
point Shall Scourch the
audience - the ~~ovisual~~ visual shall
blind the audience. and
I run for the falling witch
and we make love ... when
we reach The Climax, ~~the~~
the soul if her screams one
final Time and She ~~dies~~ dies.
I am shaking. I curse the
storm that ~~that~~ that brewed

I curse everything...
I curse and curse. And
I make a pact that I
shall take over. fuck
the world and it's peasents
and peons and parasites
with my power —— ect. ect ect.
~~end~~ of 1st half

* *[also there will a scene
    dureing ~~the~~ the raid where
a conversation will take place
such as: dig this: A certain
police man will come crashing
through the door with his
friends, right, as we

get ready to jam in. the club
the police shouts - alright
you hair lips, this is a
raid and immediatly
chops off the head of some
poor innocent head.... which
could be done with some
wax figure and very
fast camera work - there
is confusion all around and blood
there is a T.V. screen in the
CORNER
showing a cowboy and Indian
movie at the same time.
and the cop is the same
as the cowboy on the screen
and as the head tumbles

off, the head says "But we are on private grounds, doing our own thing, we are passive. we are ~~~~ n our own Loveing world." r something to this order. e camera captures all other xcitement; girls screaming onfusion and flashes to the T.V. Screen and the cow oy says as he choppes e Indian's head in half, as it rolls es, and I am ~~~~ ~~~~ Society d Law and order." appror. words. me one gets blasted ~~in two~~ in two at ~~~~ and blood splatters over

Camera lens—and the camera man gets knocked to the side. More sick. ~~cool~~ conversation, more confusion... I Take one more swig from the acid bottle, grab a few joints from a cop who found some and lit one just to see ~~how~~ if it's the good shit.... bust the bottle over his head, grab the innocent girl by the hair, & drag her through the commotion, and into a ~~~~ giant Toilet bowl labeled "your last chance for miles." or "let yourself go, Baby!"...

drinking gin....
from the bath tub
the Copa Club
Staying on Earth is such
a sin .ribby diddly doo doo. dum dum dum.

rudy doo - dupee dee
hip hip horray for LSD.
were floatin in heaven
were floatin in heaven.

then a bust comes
with cops in old cars parks
up beside stink ways and
new dated cars . cops . old uniforms
axes and clubs breaks in
2nd bust some people
regular old raid scene

Timeless bust sequence
starts off in freak out
rock group playing and
feeding back singing
"We're floating in Heaven".
light show ect...ect.....
then screen starts turning
upside down, slightly
breaking into old fashioned
faded pastel film and
the musicians playing the
Instruments of 30's.
for this 5 minute scene
we need stars and stripes
for the girls, red lipstick, type
blazer straw hats but still
some people with electric hair
pot cigarettes decked out

Jimi with Jeanette Jacobs backstage at Shrine Auditorium, Los Angeles, February 10, 1968 (Copyright © 1993 Flower Children Ltd/Chuck Boyd)

Jimi with Jeanette Jacobs backstage at Singer Bowl Auditorium, New York City, August 23, 1968 (Tom Monaster)

Carousel Theatre, Framingham, Massachusetts, August 25, 1968
(Copyright © 1993 Leonard Eisenberg)

"On the desert sands, I rest my weary head . . ." Hawaii, October 4, 1968

Winterland, San Francisco, October 11, 1968 *(Baron Wolman)*

Minneapolis Auditorium, November 2, 1968 *(Mike Barich)*

Boston Garden, November 16, 1968 *(Copyright © 1993 Leonard Eisenberg)*

Woolsey Hall, Yale University, New Haven, Connecticut, November 17, 1968 *(Joe Sia)*

Philharmonic Hall, New York City, November 28, 1968 *(Jeffrey Mayer/Starfile)*

Jimi in the George Frederic Handel House, London, January 1969
(Barrie Wentzell/Starfile)

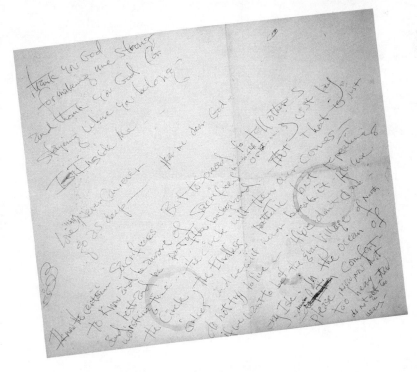

Handwritten note (top left)

(meeting with Jimi) Thurs. 4/17/67

to Name either: Sky Stepping Research.
~~Star Note Studios~~ or
Rhythm Cake Inc.
Electric Temple

Please: another copy
of Dylan Tape as ~~soon~~
soon as possible —

Please draw $1500 — for me
today if possible
[MUS-PPR 3]

Typed memo (right)

April 22, 1969

M E M O

TO: JIMI HENDRIX AND MIKE JEFFERY

FROM: JIM MARRON

RE: PURCHASE OF AMPEX TAPE MACHINES FOR STUDIOS I &

           Michael Hecht has completed
negotiations for the purchase of Ampex Tape Machines
for Studios I & II. The agreement he has reached
with Ampex requires a 20% deposit on the order with
a balance due over a three-year period:
TOTAL PURCHASE PRICE - $84,000.

           Please sign below as authorization
for a transfer of funds.

                    * * * *

           WE HEREBY AUTHORIZE Michael
Hecht to transfer the amount of $17,000 to Electric Lady, Inc
to provide for the above-mentioned deposit on Ampex Tape.
Machines for Studios I & II.

_____
Jimi Hendrix

_____
Michael Jeffery

Handwritten note (bottom left)

Songs to try in Studio.

1. Have you heard
2. Have you ever ~~had that feeling~~
3. Finish Izabella...
4. ~~What~~ Send my love to the universe
5. Machine Gun — (vocals and 2nd lead guitar)
6. Burning Desire...
7. Feeling Wine -
8. Valleys of Neptune - Arising
9. Power of God --- Love to Devon

the sky just fell down
and as I seen she had
stardust in her eyes, Jeanne Eagels.

(Nona Hatay)

Madison Square Garden, New York City, May 18, 1969 *(Nona Hatay)*

Red Carpet Inn

615 E. MOREHEAD ST. / CHARLOTTE, N. C. 28202

1.

"as long as you want to
believe the world is
a stage, then appoint
me, your electric
stage hand... And I
shall produce
upon you, An
over welming hurricane
and sling you through
to the VAST middle
and let your body
there tremble
~ but force to stand.
the middle, as
calm as an
baby's brain.
I shall let it
drain away
your nerves.
And take my
finger, and
scrape
around
the edge
of the bowl and in
your sub conciouse ear I shall serve

Return this chute frozen

2.

And what
you will
witness will
not be from
my limbs direct,
but by proxy.
Straight from
your own script
you have your
own devils toll —

It shall scorch the
pale edge of your outside
which has no reality
side at all... But that's
the one part of your script
but not alone, it
belches from hell ...
Are you satisfied,
or do you want to
stay the limit? Since
the game must obey
the supporting role
... that you by
unnatural means
invented, I'll
make you
witness the
taste of
your own

3.

Child ruthless screaming
walls... See your children outside
the swirling hurricane with
your blurred tears, laughing at your vision keen.
Wonder, don't they where you learn
how to bleed and scream your home made pain.
Music goes by the rules of the present
air. listen passivly as my guitar
howls and grinds and unwinds
and dines upon the spelling of your
gue and name...
you're on stage! Hear the world
hurricane applaud... See your
reflection on your self made
stage as you are forced up to the
spinning edge. "the world is
a stage, the world is a stage"...
you fool, you forgot your lines or
cant you hear me; is the wall of
sand ripping away your ugly ledge...
into, but not quite the walls of
eternity... let's hope the meal of yourself
it will at least not digest but as a grape
may notice as a flavour... Of macaroni and
cheese old rome and coluseum lions would
even deny. But something wrong; I see
you stop and sobfully stutter... Play your

Part
of your
belief or
You shall be relied.
Does that sound refreshingly thrown
in your burning face?
EXIT; stage down in hope that
In forgetful History, mongers
the Hurricane
leaves before you
finish the off.
The world,
thank God
can act
a disgrace

Vallys of Neptune ... Ariseing—

June 7 1969

1. I feel the ocean swaying me.
Washing away all my pains.
See where I used to be wounded,
Remember the scar?
Now you cant see a thing ---
And I dont feel no pain —

Singin about the Vally of Sunsets.
Green and blue.. Canyons too
Singin' bout Atlantis love songs.
the Vallys of Neptune is a-rising!

2. Mercury liquid... Emerald's Shining;
Telling me where I came from—
Honey Sun ... Tourquise Bed he
lays in ---... on the Burning
edge Horizon-

I'm Sailing on.-- the Bluebird
mission --- Bubble and Cur
and tiptoes in the foam -
See the wind make love to all
the ocean... Joy spread and
the message got home —

Singin about the Vally of Sunsets
Purple and gold... the Atonues of the l
Before About ancient Egypt, there
were moon trips
the Vallys of Neptune is-ariseing

3. look out East coast, but you're
gonna have a neighbor,
A rebirth land ..
the praying Burning Sounds.

We know there were ... World's
So much older ----
And they shall rise, and
tell us much more the truth
Of man -

4. I See visions of sleeping peaks
erupting...
releasing Oreleaseing all hell that
will shake the Earth from end to end -
And this aint Bad news, good news,
or any news ... It's just the throth,
Better Save your souls while
you can —
Sing in about the New Vallys
of the sunrise ... Rain bow cleen,
the world is gonna be...
Singing about getting Reedy for the new TIDE
the vallys of Neptune is-ariseing.

I excaped from the Roman
Coluseum...
        May 18, 1969 —

As I reached the
same by way of
of flying night
Bird   I layed down my gun
            to relax ... I decided to play
with time my old friend, time !

Then all of a sudden
Jesus took on through the
            mirror just ahead of me

I said what brings you here, today?
He said ... I heard my name
mentioned as I was passing along
the way ... And I figured this
was a good time to say something
what I forgot The last time — you know, what I meant to say,
                    That's when I realized that he was as spaced out as me.

Something about women being
the whole 2 1/2 of today
    And not being treated the way
they should . Well It's understood.
    I said, as I passed them
another glass of vintage A D 02 wine .
    I said This is 69   what a year
for the snow to fly

LONDONDERRY HOTEL
PARK LANE LONDON W1

Telephone 01-493 7292
Telex 263292
Cables Londhotel London W1

            Love is trying
        thank the Lord —
        thank the Lord —
Our Moon is wonded crying —
It bleeds a sword
It bleed's a infants sword

        And you look out your
        window and the noise and
grass   of life —
bustle
        It is not screaming for today
        It is not made for today —
                    made for
    And the visions of Earth tears—
    the rivers of futures being born—

71

Chant: Ball and chain for sale
Master's gone to hell

HOTEL *Navarro*
ON-THE-PARK   July 19, 1969
112 central park south, new york, n.y. 10019
212 circle 7-7900
Cable NAVARROTEL

Cowbell Beat

1. You got me sitting up on the shelf
while you're out bewitching someone else
Do I live, Do I die
Do I laugh, Do I cry,
What game am I spose to lose in this Time?

2. You got chains attached to my head
You spreading magic honey all in your bed
what is it you want just
a puppet that talks
or mabye just a lover who makes love to the dead.

Bridge: Step onto the stage.. Just for a few 2 minutes.
let's see what Kind of Juggler, you really are
Say, without that whip and those Bloody Boot's,
which are rented.. You actually could become

a morning Star..

Talk: But you rang your last bell
Even your planets, they've gone to hell
And your world turns to nothing but a bubble
in a shot gun Jar.

— *(second page)* —

arro July 19, 1969
ON-THE-PARK
112 central park south, new york, n.y. 10019
212 circle 7-7900
Cable NAVARROTEL

And now you don't know Who you really are.
this music slower, softer,

3. So instead of trying to make me your slave
Why don't you Just... call it a day.
Either way I'm gonna win
So save yourself some wind
Don't make me be the last to see
You to your grave) ...

(Back to chant:)

well well, Ball and chain ... for sale.
New Day Holidays come ... Masters gone to Hell...
well, well Ball and chain ... for sale.
Sunrise comes ... Master's dying in Hell ..
ect...

Honolulu, Hawaii, May 30, 1969 *(Robert Knight)*

As I look into my crystal ball... there
was formed a tragedy —
Oh But there's nothing to worry about...
It was just a flash from my memory —
Well it seems that the Holiday Wheel
you know, the one that was between Earth
and the moon — Well any way there was
2,000,000 killed.. Bodies floating in the
afternoon —

Explosion; 1,000 or more, announcing
tidal waves and Hurricanes —
And down on Earth we lost 3 continents
their firey soul & snuffed out by
Nature's ice and rains —

And pieces, of my life —
floating still soaring through space —
But my sons and wifes.
landed on Mars to start another race)

As I gazed upon my crystal ball
there formed a cloud of jealousy —
But there's nothing to feel sad about
By this Time, it's only history —
Well it seems that the Chambers of the
Gods were being emptied for good.
Why would such heavenly beings would war
to desert Earth — But as I watched
I understood.

As the clouds turned to a Jealous
Green, which was concieved in the heart
of man — the people didn't respect
the help of the Gods. Instead they turned against
immortal man — As they tried to defy, they
died, into the wicked pits of Hell —
Diana wept a Tear after we made love)
and said my Earthly Darling, I must bid
you fare well — the fate of your mud brothers

As pieces, of my life,
floating still soaring, in Space
She could have been my wife.
But her time, I didn't dare wish
to waste —

As I stared into my Crystal ball
there was formed a Tearing of hearts.
Ego Armies marched gently into view —
Only to be blown apart. —

As the sun whispered it's secret false
through space... to men thinking the pride
opposite — Telling them that it was
Such a disgrace to think that men were
the ruler of it — well you know
how the story goes — the sun they thought
was thier circling Slave

74

round and round and round the
tables she goes — Some Carried
the thought right to thier grave.
And I smell the scorch of the
burnt out minds ... who searched
for the hurting truth of space. And the
dizzeness they felt inside —
reflected off the spinning
slave pebble earth —

As fragments, of my life
Some floating, some soaring in space
collections, of my soul
will turn complete only as time will age.

As my tears drop on my crystal ball,
signifies the reflections of Christ —
As I blink, His angels take him away

What he said, man trys to self
disquise. Well he held a book with
help from God. As reward, He
wipes our blood from his eyes.
And the cross that he would
use for his throne — represents
not life but death — IS this the way
all heros go. Carrying the first necklace
of death — His preaching the belief
of eternal Happiness to rest.
or were his angels just UFOS
blinding those vapor trails lead from
Another light year land —
or was it really tomorrow's daydreams daydream —
blemished by the smudgey finger
prints of man —

And slivers, of my life
floating, still soaring in space
And spirits of Beehives
even they find a resting place.

As I wander through my crystal ball
I ride upon the waves of sound —
I see platforms of launching
pads even before the first blade of
grass turned brown —
And I taste thier tunnels, through
the sky — As the axis turns in it's womb.
frozen flowers and animals try to
hold positions they had before
thier morning bloomed —
And I follow the last rocket up —
to the library of the Moon's meadows.

Newport Pop Festival, June 22, 1969 *(Globe Photos)*

from th middle of a tomb whose lights
burn only for survival...
our tired bodies finally understands obeys ~~our~~ Beating hearts

Meet me in the Country
Meet me in the Country
the city's breath is getting
~~a~~ way too evil to breathe ●
Meet us ~~t~~ in the Country
~~that s~~ leave the pigs and
rats in the City —
Under the Gypsy Sun, we
All will ~~s t k~~ clearly Reach the ~~Grace~~
Do Beat of ~~God~~ living....to Give and Recieve WITH LOVE AND EASE ●

2. We'll Dance to the drums
of the ~~doom of Open~~ OPEN Life....
Love is the Rythym of ~~Fing~~
Man and Wife...

Faith in the Beat for everyone
God ~~breaks~~ Music ... ~~through~~ the life of the
Gypsy Sun ....
Diffrent Beat: Of the Grand Canyon World and
the prairies...
through the endless ● fields and valleys
... Mother Earth mountains Her
breasts and ~~of Spirits~~
Crystal fountains ... water falls

Songs for Woodstock —

- Beginning — intro   E
- Message to universe   D
- Getting My Heart together   E
- ~~Ezes~~   D
- Gypsy Woman — A
- IZABELLA   G
- ~~Easy Lady~~ Slow Blues —   B
- ~~Red~~ Lover Man — B
- Master Mind — ~~B~~ D

GYPSY SUNS RAINBOW —
Right before
the Morning's
Came to Earth

A. 1. 500,000 Halos   Unfinished Rough sketch of woodstock fest.
   out shined the mud and ~~History~~
B. We washed and drank in
   ~~~~ ....in God's tears of Joy,
   And for once ...and for everyone —
   the truth was not a mystery —

2. Love called to all ...Music is Magic.
   As we passed over the walls of Nay   and beyond
   Hand in Hand as we ~~lived~~ and   made real
   ~~over came~~ the dreams of Men —   Peace at last
   We came to ~~gather~~ ... Danced with
   the pearls of Rainy weather
   Riding the waves of Music and
   Space ... Music is Magic ...
   magic is life ...
   ~~love~~ Love As never Loved Before —
   Harmony to Son and Daughter ... man and Wife —

Woodstock, August 18, 1969 *(Copyright © 1993 Leonard Eisenberg)*

Harlem, New York City, September 5, 1969 *(Douglas Kent Hall)*

(Bill Nitopi Collection)

Have you heard — what the
wind's blowing round.
Have you heard — the all
the people is coming right on
down —
Communication ... is coming on
strong —
it don't give a damn ... if your
hair is short or long —
get out of your grave —
Everybody is dancing in the
street —
Do what you know (and don't be shor)
practice what you preach

you got to tell the children the
truth ... they don't need a
whole lot of lie's ...
Because one of these
times they'll be running thing
So when you give them love, right
So when you give them
Love ... You better make it right —
Woman and child, man and wo
The Best love to Have is the love
of Life —

Cause it's time for you and
me ... Come to face reality —
forget about the past Babe ...
things aint what they use
to be — (keep it straight ahead) Break
we got to stand, side by side;
got to stand together and
organise —
power to the people, freedom
of the soul —
pass it on to the young and old.

Slow Blues   Sippin Time
                              Sippin' wine -

     Well I'm Sippin' wine
And don't know where to go
  People, tell me lies —
And they really hurt me So

Drinking wine ---
Got a plane to catch to where
Don't know, where to hide
~~Aint no rest~~ ... Aint no one to really care

Turn the radio on - ..
Oh But now, I have to leave.
Just a fool to cry for them.
Specially when they ~~stare~~ laugh at me

(BRIDGE)
Well ... Sawdust floor
Don't every Stick to my shoes
try to ... make them Smile
          while they make me Blue

     Well I'm ~~not~~ sipping wine
On a lonely crowded Jet -
Knowing all the time
~~test all Diet seat and test~~ ...
I'm a fool who aint learned yet.

Drown in Wine
Am I drowning love?
I ~~heard~~ see ~~that~~ that word fly by.
Written in the clouds above

Drown in Wine
Cant be late for the Show
I see love fly by
Written in the clouds below.

World T.V   the world's
                             a T.V.

                             And Hang ups
                             are commercials.

1. I'm traveling a speed
unknown to man
and I carry love for all
in the mirror of my hand.

words
and
music
J. Hendrix

2. I say Love for all -- don't try to run
away ...
look at the mirrors of your heart.
face the thruth today —

chorus. I am what I am thanks God
Some people don't understand
Help them God -
I say find your self first g
and then your Tool -
I say find yourself first, don't
you be no fool -

3. Here comes a woman
Sweat all down Her back
for Birth or pleasure, she's
on the right track ..
But for being free
she aint suppose to plea.
and don't rely on no man -
to try and understand -
I say find your self first
and then your Talent.
Work hard in your mind
for it to come alive .
and then prove to the man
That you're as strong as him
cause in the eyes of

Jimi with the Voices of East Harlem, Fillmore East, New York City, December 31, 1969 *(Copyright © 1993 Amalie Rothschild)*

God ...you're Both children
to him ...
You are what you are Thank God
You Gonna Shine like a Star
with the help of God —
But we find our selfs first
and then our Tool ...
find your self first don't be no
                        fool

(Amalie Rothschild)

86

Cal-Expo Fairgrounds, Sacramento, California, April 26, 1970
(Copyright © 1970 Larry Hulst/ Michael Ochs Archives/
Venice, California)

the juke box dies, the lights go down
the saw dust floor has claimed
the last of my drinks. - intoxication
makes my eyes a fool and makes
my brain almost cease to think -
Candle light plays upon the ring
upon the hand which doesn't seem
like my hand any more -
the Bar is closed, I guess I'll go
back to my little Red velvet Room on
the Basement floor -
2. A car horn interrupts my staggering
my name is called, my minds up
against a wall for a second or two
well if it isn't my old friend, says
a chuckle from within the car, I've
been looking all over for you -
My Memory beats and robs my
Smile and greetings doah
reach This man, I first came in to,
quite a while ago - A lot has changed,
and I still walk towards the little
Red velvet room on the Basement
floor -

Hotel Elysée
60 EAST 54TH STREET
NEW YORK 22, N. Y.

I am your trash
man — throw out all
your trash ~~today~~
today —
Clean out your mind
today —
please pass the weed
and please take some heed
Take your fast glass
sons and
Throw them away

Hotel Elysée
60 EAST 54TH STREET
NEW YORK 22, N. Y.

there he goes, Hey
I just the Gypsy Bandit.

Hotel Elysée
60 EAST 54TH STREET
NEW YORK 22, N. Y.

Gypsy talk —
She has been here
3 times and the
4th Time, she was
emptied in from the
mouth of a Bottle —

Hotel Elysée
60 EAST 54TH STREET
NEW YORK 22, N. Y.

Seems like I seen you
some where before —
And her dog named pig
had a red neck shaped
just like a cracker —
dipped in rot hole

Hotel Elysée
60 EAST 54TH STREET
NEW YORK 22, N.Y.

Slow Blues
With Harmony
#Solos.

With ~~a line~~

Address 3rd trash
can from the left. that's
where I'll be —
Just take all your blues
and throw them at my
feet. — Oh that's
what friends are for

Beautiful Banquet Facilities Available For All Functions
Please call Banquet Manager for Further Information

Hotel Elysée
60 EAST 54TH STREET
NEW YORK 22, N.Y.

Yes I sing the blues
for me and you.
Let me do changes
~~so it~~ and come back and
tell you. So it won't
be so hard when it's time
for you to go through.

Beautiful Banquet Facilities Available For All Functions
Please call Banquet Manager for Further Information

---

anything
is possible
after an
embarrassing
situation —

And once you ~~take~~ take
out all that rubbish
and hate and —
load it on my truck
But don't make me
work late — I am
your trashman —
And don't ~~forget~~ I also

want to live —
not just survive —
~~And we burn up all your trash no later than 5:00~~
I aint your Black
slave — Just because
I just might try to wash out
your mind — Its up to
you friend —
To get up off your rusty
behind

~~Pass the peace weed~~
and
Please pass me the peace
weed, ~~and~~ take some
heed — throw all that MIXED UP
speed away — All that
dirt is gonna clog and
hurt — man you'll reach
100 yrs old in a day —
I am your trashman

I am your trash man —
I come to keep your
houses clean
I am the trashman
Take out all your ~~dusty~~ Dirty
Blues and dreams —
Well when I come
around to collect for
the Bill

Hotel Elysée
60 EAST 54TH STREET
NEW YORK 22, N.Y.

that's when I come
around for my pleasure
kill...
I am the trash man
You must have seen
me in private your T.V.
Guitar and voice Break

Hotel Elysée
60 EAST 54TH STREET
NEW YORK 22, N.Y.

I'm here to clean up—
All your hang ups
or come downs I'm
gonna kill...
that is my duty.
So please don't try to make
me crawl up no hill

Hotel Elysée
60 EAST 54TH STREET
NEW YORK 22, N.Y.

may I whisper in
your ear....
Say something
you ought to hear
Lots of people so dear
they're getting hurt...

Fall 1968 (Copyright © 1970 Larry Hulst/ Michael Ochs Archives/ Venice, California)

1. May I whisper in your ear
from my heart so you'll ~~hear~~ clearly he
there ~~are~~ people so dear ...
they're like Children ...
Group→ In a ~~cold~~ naked world ...
Beautiful Children
trapped In an old World —

2. May I ~~take~~ you away
from the evils of today
to the dreams of tomorrow   Music Break with vibes and guitar
You know that Heaven ...
• Group→ Has no sorrow
We know that Heaven ...
• Group→ Has no tomorrow —
3. Hear the Sound of ~~~~ the Magic drums   -solo-
Hearts are beating for the Sun
Sending Evil on the run.
Now watch the wind ...

"The Earth giveth and breathes life and death, the moon, taketh only as servant to the flow . . . and breathes for its own, not at all." Washington Hilton Hotel, March 10, 1968 *(John Gossage)*

ASTRO MAN and STRATO-WOMAN
THE COSMIC LOVERS
OF THE UNIVERSE and anything

please understand what
I'm trying to say

I READ love the comics so It's easy
to say ——

I had a dream just the
other day
that I was... ASTRO-Man.

I'm Astro-man.... I'm flying higher than
that faggot Superman....
so ever could —— ever would-

they call me ASTRO man ...
If you signal, I'll give you a hand...
to Blow out what I can....
.... in the Rest of your Mind.

(Then thrilling suspense type music comes in
as narrator gives set-up of
scene

I've been Jesus Christ
30 twice ...

Super man —— C'mon, throw
the Dice -

Capt. Midnite —— How do I look.

King Out of sight —— write a
new Book ——

Whatelse do you have to offer
what else is up for sale

What else do you want to
turn me to —— you want to

and I, this time if it's not me, myself
all you all May as well go to Hell.

106

Story about Black Boy from venus
and white girl from mars
find Love and Happiness on Earth
To Gather

And Send my love to Kathy
a Goddess of All Beauty galore
I would be Over daring ...to ask
for your precious LIFE TIME...
All the Love that lives Centuries of Depth
for the Love inside which
Has Not been touched or tasted...
Is So Much ENOUGH for the vast armies of Angels
that protect us...
I'll always wonder Would it carry enough patience
for such a lost soul as myself.

Give me back my life
and I'll send you back your
wife --- It doesn't make
too much difference either way to me
By this time, Both are dying
And Who Knows ... I may Throw in
a little crying -- But you'll pay
anything extra, I'll guarentee
Her and I are just layin, waiting to be set free

Also send my love to Joana Larks
let me tell you about a self proclaimed
the story of tom duley queen

I split her neck with the sound
of Help... Her Hair ...it
already was the color of
her response ... As she crawled
drunk with out of my TAVERN door.
death
One nite of pearly night amidst the stables
of Navarro... She all but
dry drained my fountains
dry... So I'm left with out
tears of sorrow... to mix
with the blood flowing Of the floor.
quietly through the boards
Only just enough moister left
to moisten my ever LOVE BLINDED
eye ---
And this is a story ... she will
forget to tell for others in other words
Her essence died with her in Hell...
all is well ...all is well...
thank Heaven for Hell
thank Heaven for Hell ---

107

Hell to Heaven
Heaven to Hell
Please Send
Deirhor
~~And Same~~ Angel
to Love me Now.

to Hell with Heaven
to Heaven ~~with Hell.~~

Unless you don't
send me Somebody
to Love... The Truth
of you Both - I'm
gonna Tell. STOP!
                LOUD

I'u never fall in Love
and I shall never cry.
That's what the Witches
Tell me
Because if I ever do,
~~I~~ A part of me is
Sure to die ...
that's what the
witches tell me.

And you know for
~~With~~ witches are Bitchs.

Pass it on

① LONDONDERRY HOTEL
PARK LANE LONDON W1
Telephone 01-493 7292
Telex 263292
Cables Londhotel London W1

I aint always done right.
That don't mean you can always
Keep doing wrong pass it on ____
                    Pass it on ─

I climbed mountains and
Mountains fell on me
But that don't mean I'm as
weak as I use to be
          Pass it on Pass it on.

I blew Dreams through a
Pipe of Steam ... But that
don't mean I'm a drag machine P.1.0
                                et.

Pass it on ② LONDONDERRY HOTEL
PARK LANE LONDON W1
Telephone 01-493 7292
Telex 263292
Cables Londhotel London W1

the world is trembling
breaking, shaking, Heavy
Love making ... the Stage is
cleared for the Stars ... the
and the
GODS ... pass it on, pass it on
Angels come to come and came
and now they're trying
to be gone ..... Pass it on ...Pass it
                                   on

GOD help the Understanding
of love and sweat ...
Day and Night ....
rejoice and regret ... pass it on ─

one kiss faf yur eyes

LONDONDERRY HOTEL
PARK LANE LONDON W1

Telephone 01-493 7292
Telex 263292
Cables Londhotel London W1

1. The path leads Through into
your eyes ... into your warmth,
through down into the jungles
of your wandering's ....
Your needs to save and be saved
from yourselves as crocodilles upon
thier backs, we hand in hand
Shall Tip-toe across thier sleeping slowness
reaching the wings of birds of
paridise from your heights as I
with My New found companion;
Continue to follow the path
into the ALL SUNRISE —

the Harder The Rain falls ...
The more the heart calls ... upon
the easy rivers of hopeless
to be swept away ...
pre-maturely —
weather the storm and
as the last lightning Tears
Our skies ... The Birth of
Clearness Dance upon our naked
EYES — stripped to only faith
as Harvest rippens as it drinks
So do we — I must Come to think.

110

St. Paul Auditorium, St. Paul, Minnesota, May 3, 1970 *(Mike Barich)*

Moon life in Spiral light —

1.

Moon lite ... Bathe US in
Silver flight — trips as they
breath of air ... Quick ~~as~~ as acid
of life ...
life upon the grasses...moist...only
Mother Moon whispers the final
Command of orgasm ... purpose
of comeing together beyond ● children.
What more keeps Men alive?
GOD? DOG? Mirrors or mirages?
Take me Moon as My Love lies in
Heat under my waiting, for I feel

(Moonlite ect.)

2.

She is real ... And this is beyond
Heaven Itself sotic) I must protect ————
for the love of Happiness for my Mate
to make reunion as One, we must
not be late .... ✪

She is Woman, young, old, wisdom
she holds in her mouth and heart
~~refreshing~~ as dew ~~as~~ oasis
quietly refresh the wanderers and
~~thanks~~ is heard from thier sighs
of relief of needs ~~they~~ thirst, not
knowing the language of the waters
and sands but rejoice as ocean
breaks it's seeds ● across the barren
land,

3. Moonlite -

o my Love hold on to me for
 once in your world at least
a moment, I am a part of ..
Needing .... wanting - Drinking
from my woman & as the Sun
drinks from the clouds of rain.
a purpose so light as rays,
  So deep as the waves —

    Waves = .. motion
              rythum ...

    Africa —

  RAYS = . Melody.
          evolution .... purpose
    +   America
 together?
a song -- Marriage of the fruit and (over)

4.
  frustrations
of the past .... the Moment of
NOW - ... Tears of Joy ... laughters
of sorrow ... And the Birth of nesesary
Dreams of tomorrow

LONDONDERRY HOTEL
PARK LANE LONDON W1

Telephone 01-493 7292
Telex 263292
Cables Londhotel London W1

the Terra Revolution
and VENUS.

1. Now ... the covering, cloudy
and hot, which is ~~wrapped~~
draped around all of visual
Venus is there, Reflecting
Sun, Takeing a small amount
letting it seep in to use as
the ultimate physical power
of ~~nukes that~~ world –

Once earlier, there was a
small passing ~~thought~~ that people
came in from the now astroid
belt; (then, a planet the approximate
Size of Earth –). Reasons for
the change to the chain of the
space rocks as they are today were
of men and ~~other~~ other life there

every thing needed to enjoy
and ~~cheat~~ and live –
It was then believed That
love itself, didnot exist
until the meeting of the races ..
or should I ~~say~~, worlds –
Not appreciating the perfect values
and liveing ~~conditions~~,
the Race of people from this
planet ex~~perimented~~ played
with God, played with the Idea
of not travelling to another world
by rocket, but by planet –
they built Rockets the size
of Maine on the so-called
eastern side of the planet –
they tried moving or ~~changing~~ altering
the whole orbit of thier life
embelical cord ... unaccording to
the natural Rythm God had planned

God; meaning absolute
Energy .. ◎ the Sun -

When your Body itches at
a Certain area; you ~~scrat~~
Scratch that ~~area~~ area -
the Sun reacted and
the magnet upset destroyed
the world known as it's)
normal state - - - At least
it has been thought that
the people were forwarned,
left, (~~the~~ few of them) went to
Mars ... eventually tampered
with the natural working motion
there, upsetting this time, the
air ... As it is constantly
leaking even today, soon to
be as the cold: dead: servant moon.

These lost Souls did not know
and still do not folly realise That

We are not here alone, that
there is God besides ~~them~~ ~~up~~
the temples they shall call bodies
or vehicles; that each Stone
they touch, they Shall learn
more and more) of the purpose)
of living of Giving and
recieving - these and other
motions of live we shall
not fear to say God has been
through .. He is controller .. But
they forgot, did not believe, or
just snuffed the feelings or
thoughts off to continue with
Thier ~~crying~~ crazy soul searching
always trying not to satisfy
Thier lust and desires, but before
appreciating, they were to creat
new ones - the soul that is
pitiful lost will be drawn very close

quicksand — any kind of (watch House)
or motel for death to come
and talk, entertain, and leave.

Wait! At beginning of this
sketch, the message came to
me from Messenger waves
It seems on the stressing
information of Venus today
and Earth and her problems
Today -

Our the second stone from
Star (Venus) Has been
very busy getting ready for the
Time to communicate with
Earth to try and warn the
People of Earth of potential
Self Destruction —
which is completely against
the will and Grace of living.
These people of Venus are of
a younger trap from this astroid
womb of Humans — Love is with them
as They are closer to the Sun.

Closer to the Sun is the mission
of today — But in order for Something

to realized (down into) we break things
which then has to be beat upon,
stoned, tarred and feathered,
anything and everything it must
go through to even stay abreast
with the faith of keeping it in
light and if wanted to be said
aloud to be accepted, or followed to
be Believed, it must go through
actually Hell, the spirit travels
faster than Hell.... eventually as
fast as any Heaven it sets to
realize and live in -
but going through the Battles of
carrying any belief leads
to painting. Disquisering or
masquerading or being naked —
But on Earth once you are naked
from head to toe... you are
on the what-else-is-new list and
famous and fortunatly will have
tendencies to upset or blind
or disturb. therefore Symbols,
signs, non arguments, clownery, today's
tech inques must be used.
Gods and Goddesses being
mentioned too much pulls

awareness and Bizzareness
in clash with actual Honest
communicating to who ever, or
whatever unless the point
of the whole subject itself
is ~~completly~~ completly understood
or proved... or some sort of
evidence dropped into the package.
or History sheltered mentions.

Been: On the moon ... So many traces
and lefts
on Mars ... So many places
on Venus ... So many Races
on Earth ... So many faces

Love is being tested Here -
or at least, the Love for our
WHOLE world. Not just our ~~families~~.

People must Never be afraid of paths
chosen by God. --- IN thier
hearts they see the path so much
more clearly and thoruthfully than
even the eyes - But in time, the
tempting Beautiful Body only 2s fards the

eyes will in time, come to pass.

today I burn under my Brain's
conscience of what
propels me out of trouble at times
into Time itself, outside into
the Space of it all... My Body cannot
breath there ... What is my mind
doing there? Why is my soul

Surpassing cousins, egos, security, ect,
going fast as the speed of thought.
the fastest and longest far reaching this we know
long ago - Sleepless nights world
drift in with thier bags
and books of wonderments and
self-debates... not of myself but
of Stars, music, Saturns rings
Astro-notions' — Before
L.S.D, there were Visions of
eternities... So many Blisters
un-medicated, unraped by Humane
eyes as today on all across this earth
and through this House and Home
that need not be explained to you but

to the Devil... — the truth
shall be known, to all... the Will
to accept the thruth must be fed, never suspiciously bled.
It's just that we must prepare for one
—...the amazement in how the
thruth shall be presented —
Nature shows more than
anything and it does get pretty
amazing — what's sometimes
more amazing is how people
miss the warnings of Tidal waves,
Volcanos Earthquakes - ect.
I know inside they pretend to miss the message.
We really could not care for
our children — How can you
push it back on yourself in the
long run — As we feel ...eventually
we shall be our own children —
there are souls here from Venus
that have been through several
bodies of transporation —
O transistor Feeder can you hear
me thank you — the time has
come for to be on the watch, to know
the scent, to ~~recanize~~ recanize to
Stand and visualize — Stand and realize.

Midnite -lightning
~~Striking~~
Tearing , through
the skies all around -
Wake up little Baby
Hear what the
Heaven's Shouting
about ———

1. Midnite. lightning.
flashing ... all around ~~in~~ the country house.
2. thunder ... clashing ———
~~So when~~ the fields light up on our
trees and our little dreams —
2. Love ... come and see ~~how the sky~~ and all my schemes
~~Or could it be that you're afraid to~~
feel the light upon your eyes —
8. Blue light flashing ———
Shadows leap and church bells ring mad
against the night.
Love ... please stand and watch with me
to night —
feel the Soul of thunder crash ~~it~~ in the
fields out side ..——— of our embrace —

118

St. Paul Auditorium, St. Paul, Minnesota, May 3, 1970 *(Mike Barich)*

midnite lightning LONDONDERRY HOTEL
PARK LANE LONDON W1

Telephone 01-493 7292
Telex 263292
Cables Londhotel London W1

p.2 (Bridge)

Sounds like — on the mountains
all the trucks are killing a highway.

feels like...
all the dams are breaking and surging our way.

it talks like... 1,000,000 ocean's whispers

Taste like — the Blood of the Sun
but oh lord, much more deeper

Midnite, midnite Please don't
frighten my love away

---

medium slow blues. Midnite lightning

Midnite lightning
flashing... all around my House.—
Love... please — Hold me, Hold me...

tell me why... It's crashing so close to
our trees and little scenes —
2. the church bells try ring cheers.
at 12
Blue light flashing... Shadows leap in lightning
... of nites spent... in the past
years of the Barn full of —
full of witches and ghosts of dreams.
and Happy Queens.

120

Just came back ~~Baby~~
~~Ja~~Just came back
from the Storm.
— Repeat —

I didn't Know then
but I was suffering
for my Love to keep
me warm.
Hey Baby thank you —
for Picking me up —
It was cold down
there crying rain was ~~tearing~~ me up.

the wind it woke me
up by Suprise.
~~the~~ crying Blue Rain
was burning my eyes
It is you — my love, who
Brought me in
I love you much, I'll
never ever stray form
you again

oh new love, true Blue Love
Take me over, ~~please~~ Can't stand
too much more of this Teasin'.

Oh but I gotta talk about it now
yes I got to face up to it somehow
I see my new Love up on the hill
But between Her and me there's
~~Birds~~ ~~Birds~~
a misty chill.
But this rain's gonna soak my Brain.
So As I ~~try~~ try to face the thruth of it all,
~~She~~ ~~of~~ Hope and pray that She waits
for the day I may finally Join her forever
way up over the Hill.

Atlanta Pop Festival, July 4, 1970 *(Joe Sia)*

Maui, Hawaii, July 30, 1970 (Bill Nitopi Collection)

1) She's just a nite bird
Sailing thru the nite.
She's just a nite bird
Makeing a midnite flight
~~For~~ She's flying
down to me — ~~But She~~
~~Seis~~ But tommorrow I got
to set her free
So All we got - is one
precious nite — "ditto -
2. ~~~~ Throw your
Shoes and Blues
down down under the
bed —

Just wrap me up
In your wings, ha
What I said carry me
Take me Through your
dreams - Inside your
world, I want to be -
until tommorrow No
tears will you shed -
~~~~ hold on till the
sun get out of Bed

Songs for L.P.
⇒ Strate Ahead X

1. Ezy Ryder X
2. Room fox of Mirrors X —
3. Earth Blues - Today ✓
4. Valleys of Neptune ┴
5. Have you heard - ✓
6. Cherokee Mist — instr.
7. Freedom X ✓
8. Steppin Stone ✓
9. IZA Bella ✓
10. Astro Maun X —

124

Angel come down from Heaven
yesterday --- She stayed with
me just long enough for to rescue me.
And she tells me a story yesterday -
About the ~~love~~ love between the moon
and the deep blue sea —
And then she spread her wings
High over me — And she said
'I shall ~~collect~~ (Read) you ~~tomorrow~~tomorrow'
And I said "fly on my sweet Angel.
fly on through the sky. fly on my
Sweet angel; tomorrow I hope to be by
        your side —

And sure enough this
morning comes to me — with silver
wings sillovette against the glow of
the child son rise -
And my angel she said unto me
"You're ~~have been~~ liveing through me ..
~~But there are~~ still ~~are~~ tears in your eyes -
        But why are there

forget about living in the past
My Love and try to realize
    I have come, to melt away,
    Your pain and sorrow ... forever."
And I said "fly on my sweet angel, fly on through
the sky.. fly on my sweet angel. ~~the~~ Help me
    through the sky . Help me come ~~back~~
                alive   Take me ~~to~~
                        in your life

Hit Factory, New York City, August 28, 1969 *(Jim Cummins/Starfile)*

Electric Lady Studio, New York City, August 1970 *(Fred McDarrah)*

Liseberg, Gothenburg, Sweden, September 1, 1970 *(Copyright © 1993 Bildservice)*

Beverly Rodeo Hyatt House
360 North Rodeo Drive
Beverly Hills, California

forget of my name . Remember it
only as a hand shake ...introduction
to my Belief which is God... Ride instead
the Waves of my Interpreture. Music, sound —
Hypnotic if you choose. But Thruth and
life regardless of your questionable timed
~~time~~ compromises... which
I intend to erase.... Which I will erase.
Without hint of reward as I am only
a messenger And you a Sheep in process
of evolution . Almost at Death with yourself
and On the Stair case of Birth. Soon you
may almost forget the Smell of your family ....

Well I'm up here in this
womb ... looking all
around —
I look out ~~the~~ my belly
button window, and I see
a whole lot of frowns
And I'm wondering ... if they
want me ... around —

2. well what's all the fuss
out there ... what seems to be
the sham —
Cause if they don't want me
around — Hell, I'll go back to
Spirit land —

and even take a longer rest
before coming down this
Chute again? —
Man I remember the last
time ... they were arguing
about me then.
So if you don't ... want me now,
make up your mind ... give or take
you only got ... 300 days
where and when —
Cause I aint coming this way
too much more again?

They got pills, for ills, and
$thrills and even spills
~~regardless of love or hate~~
But I think you're just a little
too late.
So I'm coming on down to this
world Daddy ... regardless
of love and hate.
... I'm gonna sit up in your
Bed mama and givin in your
face — and then I'm gonna
eat up all your chocolates

Note 1 (top left):

CUMBERLAND HOTEL Marble Arch London W1 W1H 8AB
Telephone 01-262 1234   Cables Cumberotel London W1

look aer yonder —
here comes some news —
comming down ~~the~~ like lightning...
~~electric relays and those~~
straight for me and you —
people of destruction +
~~old~~ your time is
~~hold~~ out of date...
people ~~and~~ who's liveing
crooked, better start
getting straight

Note 2 (right):

CUMBERLAND HOTEL Marble Arch London W1 W1H 8AB
Telephone 01-262 1234   Cables Cumberotel London W1

I've been ~~so~~ through
some changes, a whole
lot of re-arranges —
Been through ~~some ups an~~
downs and whole lot
of turn arounds —
I been on the shelf and
even killed myself —
1,000 times ago and
maybe 1,000 times more

Note 3 (bottom):

CUMBERLAND HOTEL Marble Arch London W1 W1H 8AB
Telephone 01-262 1234   Cables Cumberotel London W1

She said she comes from
Iceland... I told her I
~~was~~ was from the west —
She took me to the snow capped
mountains — and then she
put me through the test...
we walked across the glacier,
the horses stayed behind...
and as we laid between the
frozen valleys — we kissed
for the very first time —
And now we're stuck together

CUMBERLAND HOTEL Marble Arch, London W1 W1H 8AS
Telephone 01-262 1234   Cables Cumberotel London W1

It wasn't too long ago. But it seems
like ...years ago ... since I felt the
warm hello of the Sun.
lately thing's seem a little colder
the wind, it seem's to get a little
bolder

He's got you liveing
in the grave yards
He even makes the rats
pay the rent — -
Side by side ... He try to
make yar slide into His
own torment.
we got to ride, ride, ride,
ride that porkchop down
(Repeat)
Cause if we don't y'all
this time — we'll forever have
to carry the wieght and
a Heavy form

Now He knows he
is lonely and cancer
is eating His greedy brain
and when He finds this
y'all, the whole gonna
be in pain ... we got to
ride, ride, ride,
ride that porkchop down
BACK under the ground

Dusseldorf, Germany, January 12, 1969 *(Monika Dannemann)*

"Do not ignore the sun . . . for . . . the sun is the truth shining to be seen."
(Nona Hatay)

(slow)

the Story — of Jesus
so easy to explain -
after they crucified him,
a woman, she claimed his
name'
the story — of Jesus -
He whole Bible knows —
went all across the desert.
and in the middle he found a rose,

there should be no questions
there re should be no lies -
He was was married ever
happily after ____
for all the tears we cry —
No use in arguing ____ al
the use to man. that means
when each man falls in battle, his
soul it has to roam ____
angels ____ of heaven
flying saucers to some

made easter Sunday
the name of the Rising
Sun —
the story... is written
by (so many people who dared)
to lay down the truth —
to so very many who cared
to carry the cross
of Jesus and beyond

So easy yet so hard —
is I wish not to be alone
So I must respect my other
heart —

Oh — the story
of Jesus — is history
of you and me — No question
feeling lonely —

We will guild the light
this time with a woman in our
arms —

We as men
can't explain the reason why —
the woman's always mentioned
at the moment that we die —
All we know —
is God is by our side
and he says the word

I saw you searching to be free

the story —
of life is quicker
than the wink of an eye

the story of love —
is hello and goodbye
until we meet again

(Nona Hatay)

136